# The School Practitioner's Concise Companion to Preventing Dropout and Attendance Problems

# The School Practitioner's Concise Companion to Preventing Dropout and Attendance Problems

Edited by

**Cynthia Franklin**
**Mary Beth Harris**
**Paula Allen-Meares**

OXFORD
UNIVERSITY PRESS

2008

Oxford University Press, Inc., publishes works that further
Oxford University's objective of excellence
in research, scholarship, and education.

Oxford  New York
Auckland  Cape Town  Dar es Salaam  Hong Kong  Karachi
Kuala Lumpur  Madrid  Melbourne  Mexico City  Nairobi
New Delhi  Shanghai  Taipei  Toronto

With offices in
Argentina  Austria  Brazil  Chile  Czech Republic  France  Greece
Guatemala  Hungary  Italy  Japan  Poland  Portugal  Singapore
South Korea  Switzerland  Thailand  Turkey  Ukraine  Vietnam

Published by Oxford University Press, Inc.
198 Madison Avenue, New York, New York 10016

www.oup.com

Oxford is a registered trademark of Oxford University Press

Library of Congress Cataloging-in-Publication Data

The school practitioner's concise companion to preventing dropout
and attendance problems / edited by Cynthia Franklin, Mary Beth Harris,
and Paula Allen-Meares.
p. cm.
Includes bibliographical references and index.
ISBN 978-0-19-537057-7
1. Dropouts—United States—Prevention.   2. School attendance—United States.
I. Franklin, Cynthia. II. Harris, Mary Beth. III. Allen-Meares, Paula, 1948-
IV. Title: Concise companion to preventing dropout and attendance problems.
LC143.S276 2008
371.2'913—dc22      2008018230

9 8 7 6 5 4 3 2 1

Printed in the United States of America
on acid-free paper

# Preface

School-based practitioners are frequently called upon to improve the attendance of students and to develop programs and strategies for dropout retrieval and prevention. Preventing dropout and attendance problems has never been more important than it is in the performance-driven school environments of the 21st century. High attendance standards are set and enforced regardless of a student's personal challenges or life difficulties. Low attendance in school often leads to serious consequences for students, parents, and schools who are held accountable to maintain compulsory attendance laws and policies. When searching the literature for educational practices that might work with students at-risk to dropout, school professionals have told us that they are overwhelmed with the amount of information that exists on the topics of attendance and dropout prevention. Professionals seeking answers find themselves swimming in an endless sea of various approaches and perspectives. However, practitioners are asking, what are the nuts and bolts of researched-based information concerning the best practices to be implemented? *The School Practitioner's Concise Companion to Preventing Dropout and Attendance Problems* is a book designed to provide easy access to best practice interventions for attendance and dropout problems.

## Contents of this Book

*The School Practitioner's Concise Companion to Preventing Dropout and Attendance Problems* was developed with the practicing school professional in mind. This companion book offers targeted content on how to improve school attendance and engage and retrieve students who are leaving school prematurely. Contents of this book provide easy-to-read practice information, including case studies, and practice guidelines to use when intervening with students, families, and school systems. Chapters in this book offer timely reviews of effective programs and interventions for increasing school attendance, working with under-achievement and school failure, designing alternative schools for dropout prevention, solution-focused techniques for engaging students prone to dropout, and guidelines for conducting home visits (an approach used to build relationships and engage students and families that are alienated from the school). In addition, chapters discuss strategies for working with student populations that are at high risk for dropping out (e.g., American Indians foster children, pregnant and parenting adolescents). Each chapter further follows a practice-friendly outline that includes the headings *Getting Started, What We Know, What We Can Do, Tools and Practice Examples*, and *Points to Remember*, thus providing a quick reference guide to information.

The *School Practitioner's Concise Companion to Preventing Dropout and Attendance Problems* is one of four companion books that were created to equip school professionals to effectively take action on social and health issues, and mental health problems that are confronting schools. All four books in this series offer a quick and easy guide to information and solutions for today's pressing school problems. The content for the companion books was developed using chapters from Oxford's popular resource volume, *The School Services Sourcebook*. In contrast, to the exhaustive and comprehensive *Sourcebook*, the briefer companion books were designed to provide succinct information for those who want to address a particular topic.

## Objectives of the Companion Books

When planning the concise companion books we had three main objectives in mind. Our first objective was to provide a series of affordable books whose content covered important and timely topics for school-based practitioners. We wanted the companion books to be like a search command on a computer where a quick search using a keyword or phrase can selectively lead you to the information you need. Each companion book contains updated knowledge tools and resources that can help practitioners quickly access information to address a specific problem area or concern. The second objective was for this book to communicate evidenced-based knowledge from research to practice but to do so in a way that practitioners could easily consume this knowledge. As editors, we wanted each chapter to be applied, providing practice examples and tools that can be used in day-to-day practice within a school. A third objective was to create a practical book that school practitioners could use daily to guide their practices, prepare their presentations, and answer questions asked to them by teachers, parents, and administrators. For this reason, each chapter in this concise companion book on attendance and dropout prevention provides quick reference tables, outlines, practice examples, and Internet resources for consultation.

## How the Topics Were Selected

There are many important concerns facing today's schools and you may be wondering why we chose to address attendance and dropout issues instead of a dozen other problem areas? School professionals who helped us create the timely topics addressed in this companion book provided selected topics. The original chapter topics in this book were identified through feedback from school social workers in six regions of the country. Social workers in California, Georgia, Michigan, New Mexico, Oregon, and Texas communicated with us through e-mail questionnaire, individual interviews, and focus groups. We asked about the overall challenges of working in a school setting. We asked about the most urgent and frequent problems school social workers and other practitioners encounter with students and families. School practitioners told us, for example, that their practice requires knowledge and skills for addressing attendance and dropout problems. A primary aspect of their work is direct services to individuals (school staff as well as students), to groups, and to families. Practitioners further told us that they need information on how to work with school professionals to interpret educational policies and design effective programs for dropout prevention.

## Acknowledgments

First and foremost we want to thank the Oxford University Press for supporting this work. Our deepest gratitude goes to Joan H. Bossert and Maura Roessner for their help and guidance in developing the companion books. In addition, we are thankful to Dr. Albert Roberts who gave us the inspiration and support to develop resource books for practitioners. We would further like to thank all the team of professionals that worked on *The School Services Sourcebook*—Melissa Wiersema, Tricia Cody, Katy Shepard, and Wes Baker, and our editorial board. Finally, we give credit to all the school social workers and school mental health professionals who participated in our survey and to all those who informally gave us feedback on what topics to cover.

Cynthia Franklin, PhD
*The University of Texas at Austin*

Mary Beth Harris, PhD
*Central Florida University*

Paula Allen-Meares, PhD
*The University of Michigan*

# Contents

# Contents

# Contributors

**David R. Dupper, PhD**
*College of Social Work*
*University of Tennessee, Knoxville*

**Cynthia Franklin, PhD, LCSW, LMFT**
*Stiernberg/Spencer Family Professor in*
*    Mental Health*
*School of Social Work*
*University of Texas, Austin*

**Dorie J. Gilbert, PhD**
*Associate Professor*
*University of Texas, Austin*

**Mary Beth Harris, PhD**
*Associate Professor*
*School of Social Work*
*University of Central Florida*

**Johnny S. Kim**
*Graduate Student*
*School of Social Work*
*University of Texas, Austin*

**Mary M. McKay, PhD**
*Professor*
*Department of Psychiatry*
*Mt. Sinai School of Medicine*

**Mary C. Ruffolo, PhD**
*Associate Professor*
*School of Social Work*
*University of Michigan*

**Gary L. Shaffer, PhD**
*Associate Professor*
*School of Social Work*
*University of North Carolina, Chapel Hill*

**Gail H. Sims, PhD**
*Program Coordinator*
*Community Education*
*Austin Independent School District*
*Austin, Texas*

**Calvin L. Streeter, PhD**
*Meadows Foundation Centennial*
*    Professor in The Quality of Life in*
*    The Rural Environment*
*School of Social Work*
*University of Texas, Austin*

**Dorian E. Traube, LCSW**
*School of Social Work*
*Columbia University*

**Stephen J. Tripodi, MSSW**
*Graduate Research Assistant*
*School of Social Work*
*University of Texas, Austin*

**Barbara Hanna Wasik**
*William R. Kenan, Jr., Professor*
*School of Education*
*University of North Carolina, Chapel Hill*

The School Practitioner's Concise Companion
to Preventing Dropout and
Attendance Problems

# 1 Increasing School Attendance

## Effective Strategies and Interventions

*Johnny S. Kim*
*Calvin L. Streeter*

## Getting Started

### Improving School Attendance Through Multilevel Interventions

Improving student attendance is a major preoccupation for many schools across the country. Though little educational research has focused on the relationship between attendance and student performance, some studies suggest that school attendance and student academic performance are closely associated (Borland & Howsen, 1998) (see also Chapters 2 and 3). The assumption is that when students are not in school, they cannot learn. Though this assumption seems plausible, the implied causal ordering of the relationship is not always clear. For example, does school attendance improve academic performance or does academic performance serve as an incentive for successful students to regularly attend school? Whatever the association, it has led many school districts, school administrators, and state governments to spend tremendous resources to carefully monitor, document, and report school attendance data.

Epstein and Sheldon (2002) suggest that improving school attendance is as important as any issue that schools face today. Concern about school attendance may focus on truancy and chronic absenteeism, as when students fail to come to school on any given day. But class cutting, where students come to school to be counted but then selectively skip one or more classes each day, is seen by some a symptom of alienation and disengagement from schools and a serious issue for many urban school districts today (see Fallis & Opotow, 2003; also see Chapter 3 for a discussion of dropout prevention using alternative schools and solution-focused therapy). Either way, school attendance is a serious issue and one that requires multilevel strategies to effectively address.

Truancy has been identified as a significant early warning sign that students are headed for potential delinquent activity, social isolation, and educational failure (Baker, Sigmon, & Nugent, 2001; Loeber & Farrington, 2000). Poor attendance means that students are not developing the knowledge and skills needed for later success. In addition, when not in school, many students become involved in risky behaviors such as substance abuse, sexual activity, and other activities that can lead to serious trouble within the legal system (Bell, Rosen, & Dynlacht, 1994; Dryfoos, 1990; Huizinga, Loeber, & Thornberry, 1995; Rohrman, 1993). For many youths, chronic absenteeism is a significant predictor of dropping out of school (Dynarski & Gleason, 1999). Beyond its immediate consequences for students, truancy can have significant long-term implications for youths in terms of their becoming productive members of the community. For decades, research has shown a correlation between poor school attendance and problems later in life, such as criminal activity, incarceration, marital and family problems, trouble securing and maintaining stable employment, and violent behavior (Catalano, Arthur, Hawkins, Berglund, & Olson, 1998; Dryfoos, 1990; Robins & Ratcliff, 1978; Snyder & Sickmund, 1995).

Though individual students are often blamed for truancy, school attendance may be seen as an important indicator of how well the school is functioning and the kind of educational environment created within the school. For example, large schools where students are more anonymous often have more attendance problems than small schools where a missing student is more likely to be noticed (Finn & Voelkl, 1993). In addition, students are more likely to skip school when the school environment is perceived to be boring or chaotic, when students don't feel they are being intellectually challenged, or when there are no consequences for being truant.

For schools, the consequences of truancy can be significant as well. Not only is student attendance seen as one indicator of school performance, in most states money is tied directly to student attendance. Because funding formularies often include student attendance, fewer students in the classroom mean fewer resources for academic programs. School administrators and all those involved with schools have a vested interest in getting children to school and keeping them there all day.

Truancy has important consequences for the community, too (Baker et al., 2001). These include a workforce that lacks the basic knowledge and job skills needed to fully participate in the labor market and contribute to the economy. This can result in increased costs of social services and higher rates of poverty. Local businesses are often concerned about direct losses incurred from truants' shoplifting and indirect losses from their hanging out near their businesses and fighting, using drugs and alcohol, and intimidating customers.

Thus truancy has both immediate and far-reaching consequences for individual students, families, schools, and communities. Effective interventions must understand the problem from multiple perspectives and address the problem at multiple levels.

## What We Know

Most of the research literature on low school attendance has focused either on its causes or its relationship to academic performance (Corville-Smith, Ryan, Adams, & Dalicandro, 1998; Lamdin, 2001). Despite the fact that absenteeism is a concern for schools, parents, social workers, and counselors, very little research has been done to examine ways to improve school attendance (Epstein & Sheldon, 2002; Lamdin, 2001). This is especially the case when looking for evidence-based research on absenteeism and school attendance.

Some research studied schools that offer rewards or monetary incentives to improve school attendance. Sturgeon and Beer (1990) examined 14 years of data from a rural high school in the Midwest to see if an attendance reward of exemption from taking semester tests had decreased absenteeism. They examined the school's student attendance records from 1976 to 1979, when there was no attendance reward policy, and compared them with student attendance records from 1980 to 1989, when the attendance reward policy was in effect. Results showed a statistically significant decrease in the number of absences after the attendance reward was adopted. During the years 1976–1979, the average total absent days was 1750.5, which decreased to 912.5 during the years 1980–1989.

Reid and Bailey-Dempsey (1995) randomly assigned junior high and high school girls with academic or attendance problems to either a program that offered financial incentives for improving school and attendance performance, a program that offered social and educational services to the girls and their families, or to a control group. Both the financial incentive program and case management program modestly improved school attendance over the control group, but similar results were not seen the next year. Though there was no statistically significant difference between the financial and case management programs in terms of school attendance, academic improvements were better for students receiving case management services than for students receiving only financial incentives.

Recently Miller (2002) conducted a study to see if participation in a therapeutic discipline program would improve students' attitudes on attendance, increase attendance, and provide greater insight into solving attendance problems among students at a large suburban high school. Students who were truant were randomly assigned to either the therapeutic discipline program or to a control group. The therapeutic program required students to work through a bibliotherapeutic learning packet and attend a follow-up exit conference with the dean to go over the packet. Traditional methods were used on the control group: threatening students with further disciplinary measures and in-school suspension in which students were required to do schoolwork. Both programs required students to participate in a written exercise to measure insight into ways they could help solve their truancy problems. Results from this study showed students in the therapeutic program increased class attendance, had fewer absences from classes, and listed a greater number of insights into resolving their attendance problems.

# What We Can Do

## A Multilevel Approach to School Attendance

Across the country, hundreds of thousands of students are absent from schools each day. Many times that number cut one or more classes after being counted as present in the school's attendance records. In order to effectively address attendance problems, school administrators, teachers, and staff must understand the problem from a multilevel perspective. Interventions that focus only on individual students may improve attendance in the short term for that one student. But it is unlikely that such interventions will have a widespread effect on attendance across the school. In addition, school attendance must be viewed as everyone's responsibility, not just that of the school's attendance officer. Figure 1.1 emphasizes the fact that although the individual student is at the center of our concern about truancy, an effective response must involve the school, the family, and the community.

School attendance can be influenced by a number of factors specific to the student. These might include drug and alcohol abuse, mental health problems, poor physical health, teen pregnancy and family responsibilities, student employment, and a lack of understanding of the long-term consequences of school failure.

Sometimes the school itself is largely responsible for truancy. School factors often include the school climate, such as school size and attitudes of teachers and administrators, lack of flexibility in meeting the needs of students with diverse learning styles and different cultural experiences, inconsistent policies and procedures for dealing with chronic truancy, inconsistent application of those policies, lack of meaningful consequences, a chaotic school culture and/or unsafe school environment, and a curriculum that is perceived as boring, irrelevant, or unchallenging.

Family factors that can affect student attendance include domestic violence and alcohol and drug abuse, inadequate parental supervision, poverty and low-wage

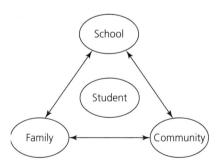

**Figure 1.1.** Student-Centered Multilevel Approach to School Attendance.

jobs that require the parents to work long hours, lack of awareness of attendance laws, and parental attitudes toward education and the school.

Communities, too, can influence school attendance. They can hurt attendance when they present few opportunities for young people or lack affordable child care or accessible transportation systems. Communities with high mobility rates and large numbers of single-parent households tend to have high truancy rates. Too, differing cultural attitudes toward education can make a difference in whether a child wants to attend school.

## Intervention Strategies
### Individual Student Strategies

Strategies that focus on the individual student tend to focus on psychoeducational interventions and cognitive restructuring (Kearney, 2003). School social workers and other counselors assess reasons a student is absent, focusing on school- and family-related issues. Cognitive and behavioral strategies can help such a student deal with anxiety, stress, and frustrations. Behavioral strategies include relaxation, imagination, and breathing exercises the student can do in class to reduce worry and nervousness (Kearney, 2003). Cognitive strategies include the use of solution-focused and cognitive-behavioral therapy techniques. School social workers and mental health professionals should also focus on increasing student's self-esteem and social skills, since most students who frequently cut school have little self-confidence academically or socially (Corville-Smith et al., 1998). After-school tutoring programs and mentoring programs can be effective strategies for students who avoid coming to school because of academic problems.

Intervention strategies that focus on students who don't like school or don't get along with a teacher or with other students are more complex and require a multilevel approach. Perhaps the strategy should focus on the student or family; are, for example, mental health services or drug/alcohol treatment services needed? Or perhaps the focus should be on academics: would these students gain more from school if it incorporated technology into the learning process and integrated vocational and school-to-work materials into the curriculum? Career internships might provide valuable hands-on experience that also further stresses the importance of attending classes. Or perhaps the focus should be on the social aspect of school: is the school one that makes students feel safe, respected, and welcomed? This can be accomplished by knowing students by name and recognizing their successes—no matter how small they may seem (Colorado Foundation for Families and Children, 2004).

This sort of multidisciplinary strategy—addressing truancy from three different sides: student, family, and school—is the only way to make long-term strides in improved school attendance. Though traditional approaches such as punishments and forcing attendance through parental involvement and truancy officers may be effective in the short run, the gains don't last.

## Family Strategies

Family involvement is an integral part of reducing school absenteeism, and schools need to collaborate with families in order to improve student attendance (Epstein & Sheldon, 2002). Family problems spill over into the classrooms and can affect student attendance and academic performance. A study by Corville-Smith et al. (1998) found that absentee students, when compared with students who attended school regularly, perceived their families as being less accepting of them, less cohesive, less consistent and effective in discipline, and more conflicted and controlling.

School social workers and other school-based practitioners are in a unique position to help families deal with their child's attendance problem. One way practitioners can assist families is by providing resources for families and students. Family problems such as unsteady employment, lack of reliable transportation, divorce, and family conflict all affect student attendance and performance. Providing resources and connecting families with appropriate social services will help reduce family problems and improve the student's attendance.

Epstein and Sheldon (2002) provides a list of three effective family strategies available to school-based practitioners:

1. *Communicate with families when students are absent.* Collaboration between the school and the family begins with frequent and open talks about the student's attendance problem. An increased effort needs to be made by practitioners to provide parents with information and resources from the school. This can be done by including the parents in school meetings with teachers, administrators, school social workers, and others either at the school or via conference call. Bowen (1999) recommends that practitioners solicit the parents' perceptions of and insights into their child's attendance problem. Bowen also recommends that school staff give parents ideas about activities and techniques they can use at home to improve their child's academic and behavioral problems. Having a specific school contact person for attendance problems can also help increase communication between the school and families if the families have that person's name and phone number (Epstein & Sheldon, 2002). This designated school employee should have resources and strategies available to help parents deal with the attendance problem.

2. *Hold workshops for parents.* School-based practitioners should conduct workshops that deal specifically with attendance problems. These workshops can provide parents with new strategies and tools to improve school attendance. Workshop topics might include reasons for absenteeism, strategies for improving attendance, advice on getting students up and ready for school on time, information on transportation resources, and tips for dealing with resistance. Workshops should

include specific information about attendance policies, procedures, and penalties to better inform families.

3. *Visit the home.* Some school social workers, nurses, and others use home visits and phone calls to parents as part of their family-based intervention to increase parental involvement in their child's schooling (Ford & Sutphen, 1996). Making home visits is an effective strategy for reducing rates of chronic absenteeism and is usually used when students have severe attendance problems. Home visits allow school personnel to gain a more ecological perspective on the student and her or his home environment; they can see if family problems may be contributing to the attendance problem. Based on the home visit assessment, practitioners can develop a contract with the family detailing specific goals that need to be met in order to avoid legal sanctions.

## School Strategies

Changes in schools' organizational structure, curricula, and culture are needed if attendance problems are to be effectively addressed (Epstein & Sheldon, 2002). Schools should promote an environment where students feel connected to the school and invested in their learning. One way to accomplish this is to improve teacher–student relationships and engage students as active members of the school community. Reducing class sizes, if possible, will increase the interactions between student and teacher and give students the attention they need. Schools can involve students in coming up with strategies and programs aimed at reducing absenteeism. By involving students and seeking their perspectives, schools help students feel important and allow their voices to be heard (Fallis & Opotow, 2003).

Some of the more common approaches schools take to address attendance problems involve referring students to school social workers and/or truant officers. This strategy can help improve attendance rates but may not be effective with chronic absenteeism. Providing attendance awards can also be helpful, but they should be given as incentives for improved attendance and not just for perfect attendance. Another strategy is to provide after-school programs that motivate students to attend school in order to participate. These after-school programs can also be educational, covering topics on improving student self-esteem and building social skills because, as we said above, absentee students more often suffer from these deficits.

The Office of Juvenile Justice and Delinquency Prevention (OJJDP) issued a report in 1998 that highlighted some of the major research findings regarding truancy. Various programs aimed at individuals, schools, and communities were funded in 1999 through the OJJDP in an effort to develop evidence-based programs aimed at improving school attendance. Table 1.1 provides an overview of each of those federally funded projects and can also be found at http://www.ncjrs.org/html/ojjdp/jjbul2001_9_1/page3. html

**Table 1.1** OJJDP-Funded Attendance Programs

| *Project Location* | *Overview of Program* |
| --- | --- |
| Department of Health and Human Services: Contra Costa County, CA | An on-site probation officer assesses ninth-graders with a history of truancy and their families. The officer will refer them to appropriate resources within the school and community. |
| State Attorney's Office: Jacksonville, FL | School district refers students and their families to the State Attorney's Office, which has a precourt diversion program when school-based interventions fail. Following the referral, a hearing is conducted with the parent, student, school attendance social worker, and volunteer hearing officer. A contract is negotiated that includes plans for reducing truancy and accessing social services and community resources. |
| Clarke County School District: Athens, GA | When students at two middle schools have five or more unexcused absences, the case manager makes home visits, calls parents, organizes parent–teacher conferences to assess the causes of truancy, and provides community and social service referrals if needed. Families who do not respond to the case management approach are summoned to appear before an attendance panel. |
| University of Hawaii: Honolulu, HI | Attendance officers in two elementary schools provide early outreach to students and their families when absences become chronic. Community resources are used to address issues that may be affecting the student and his or her family. Saturday truancy workshops are coordinated with the police department for youth with chronic truancy problems and their families. |
| Suffolk County Probation Department: Yaphnak, NY | A probation officer monitors attendance, provides help with accessing school- and community-based services if needed by the student and family to improve attendance, and observes attendance and other school-based indicators to ensure that the student's attendance and engagement at school are improving. |

*(continued)*

**Table 1.1** *(Continued)*

| Project Location | Overview of Program |
|---|---|
| Mayor's Anti-Gang Office: Houston, TX | A case manager identifies students with chronic truancy patterns in a high school. Through home visits and school-based supports, students and their families are provided with services, supports, and resources to address truancy. The program also works with community police officers who make home visits to assess family functioning, deliver information about the law and truancy outcomes, and issue official summons to the court for a truancy petition. |
| King County Superior Court: Seattle, WA | Court provides an evening workshop about truancy laws and outcomes and facilitates planning between the parent and student for addressing the cause of truancy. A school-based component was added to address prevention and early intervention in 2000. |
| Safe Streets Campaign: Tacoma, WA | The truancy project is based in one middle school, where a coordinator monitors attendance and connects students and their families with community resources to address underlying causes of truancy. |

## Key Points to Remember

This chapter recognizes the challenges that school administrators, teachers, and families face in trying to improve school attendance. Overall, the highlights of this chapter include:

• Research has shown a correlation between poor school attendance and problems later in life, such as criminal activity, incarceration, marital and family problems, trouble securing and maintaining stable employment, and violent behavior.

• Though the individual student is at the center of our concern about truancy, an effective response must involve the school, the family, and the community.

• Strategies that focus on the individual student include psychoeducational interventions, cognitive restructuring, after-school tutoring programs, and mentoring programs.

- School social workers and others may also need to encourage the use of mental health and drug/alcohol treatment services for either the student or a family member of the student.
- Family interventions include providing resources and connecting families with appropriate social services to help reduce family problems, increasing communication with families when students are absent, holding workshops for parents, and visiting parents at their home.
- Changes in schools' organizational structure, curricula, and culture are needed to address serious attendance problems.

Improving school attendance is a social problem that needs to be addressed from a multilevel approach involving not only the student and the school but also the family and community. It is also not enough just to get students to show up at school by using punitive measures such as truant officers and suspensions. Schools must work to engage the student by creating a school environment that is welcoming and by addressing academic difficulties that may deter the student from attending school.

# Enhancing Skills of Students Vulnerable to Underachievement and Academic Failure

*Mary C. Ruffolo*

## Getting Started

Many children and adolescents in educational settings today find it difficult to acquire the critical social and academic skills necessary for success in school. They are at risk of underachievement and academic failure. For these children and adolescents, the earlier they fall behind their peers, the harder it is to catch up (Durlak, 1995).

In this chapter, children and adolescents who are underachievers will be defined as students who have the critical social and academic skills but are not achieving. Underachievement can be linked to learning disabilities, behavioral difficulties, and mental-health difficulties (Deschenes, Cuban, & Tyack, 2001). Academic failure is defined as the result of a student's poor social and academic performance. Underachievement and academic failure place children and adolescents at risk for dropping out of school. Each year, approximately 23% of youth aged 17 do not graduate from high school with a diploma (Kaufman, Kwon, Klein, & Chapman, 2000). Research on some of the reasons for this place responsibility on schools and teachers. Among the factors affecting a youth's academic success and failure that are within the school's purview are class size, school size, school culture, school resources, availability of after-school help and tutoring, level of conflict and violence in the school, amount of instruction time, teachers' ability to convey care and meaning, teacher–student connections, and teacher prediction of student failure (Dimmitt, 2003).

## What We Know

Durlak (1995, p. 44), in a review of the literature on underachievement and academic failure, reports that the best single predictor of academic performance before a child reaches elementary school is the family's socioeconomic level, with many more children from the lowest income levels at risk of doing poorly. Research has repeatedly demonstrated that children whose work warrants failing a grade are very likely to have continued poor achievement and negative personal and social outcomes whether they are retained in that grade or promoted to the next (Owings & Magliaro, 1998). Children and youth of color and children and youth living in economically disadvantaged communities are disproportionately affected by these practices (Kao & Thompson, 2003; Scheurich, Skrla, & Johnson, 2000). Youth who identify as gay, lesbian, bisexual, and transgender also experience higher rates of academic failure (McFarland & Dupois, 2001).

It is critical that school practitioners address the challenge of underachievement and academic failure early. If the individual, family, school, and community factors that place a child at risk are not addressed, these children will become school dropouts (Richman, Bowen, & Woolley, 2004).

Using an ecologically based resiliency framework for understanding the complex factors that place children at risk for underachievement or academic failure will help school practitioners to assess what type of interventions can maximize their possibilities for academic success. In this framework, the interplay of risk and protective factors among individual child, family, school, peers, and neighborhood are assessed to develop interventions that promote success in school. These interventions are strength-based, developmentally appropriate, and multilevel.

Risk factors for underachievement and academic failure are conditions that contribute to barriers that may prevent a child from learning and developing. Some of the individual child and youth risk factors that can create barriers to success in school include living with chronic medical problems, having a low IQ, experiencing psychological problems, and having adjustment and temperament problems (Adelman & Taylor, 2003; Huffman, Mehlinger, & Kerivan, 2000; Richman et al., 2004). Family risk factors include poverty, violence, substance abuse, abusive caretaking, and inadequate child care provisions (Adelman & Taylor, 2003; Richman et al., 2004). School and peer factors that contribute to barriers in learning and development include poor-quality schools, negative encounters with teachers, and negative or inappropriate peer models (Adelman & Taylor, 2003; Huffman et al., 2000). Neighborhood risk factors that contribute to underachievement and academic failure include violence, presence of drug activity, minority or immigrant status, extreme economic deprivation, and community disorganization (Adelman & Taylor, 2003; Huffman et al., 2000; Richman et al., 2004).

Protective buffers in this framework are factors that prevent or counter risk-producing conditions. Some of the individual child and youth protective buffers include having a higher cognitive ability, being able to problem solve, having a sense of purpose and hope for the future, being a girl, and having an easy temperament (Adelman & Taylor, 2003; Huffman et al., 2000). Protective buffers at the family level include having adequate financial resources, living in a nurturing, supportive family, having a safe and stable home environment, having family members who completed high school, having family members who can read, and having high-quality child care (Adelman & Taylor, 2003; Richman et al., 2004). At the school and peer level, protective buffers include experiencing academic success, having a positive relationship with one or more teachers, associating with prosocial peers, having a strong bond with others, and attending a school that has a schoolwide climate that promotes nurturing and support (Adelman & Taylor, 2003). At the neighborhood level, protective buffers include having a strong local economy; having available and accessible services; living in a stable and safe community; having opportunities to successfully participate, contribute to, and be recognized by the community; and living in a community in which a child feels a sense of community (Adelman & Taylor, 2003; Richman et al., 2004).

Resilience emerges as a result of balancing the risk conditions and protective buffers across multiple system levels (Hawkins, Arthur, & Catalano, 1995; O'Keefe, 1994). Richman et al. (2004, p. 151) identify five primary areas of resiliency that promote school success: (1) social competence and connectedness (e.g., empathy and caring, prosocial peers); (2) autonomy (e.g., sense of power, impulse control, self-efficacy); (3) sense of purpose (e.g., healthy expectations, internal locus of control); (4) contextual factors (e.g., safe from bullying and school violence, accessible, supportive adults); and (5) problem-solving skills (e.g., alternative solutions, planning).

## What We Can Do

### Assessment

To assess underachievement and academic failure risks for individual students, school practitioners need to take into account the child's intellectual abilities and contextual factors (at school, in the family, with peers, and in the neighborhood). Intelligence testing, achievement testing, and testing for learning disabilities will help school practitioners to identify a child's intellectual strengths and weaknesses. The use of multiple informants (e.g., parents, teachers) and multiple methods (e.g., self-report, direct observation) in assessment is a strategy that can help the school practitioner to understand the child in context. In addition to these intelligence and achievement tests, school practitioners need to engage youth in assessment processes that capture how they perceive their family, peers, school, and neighborhood. Though a number of assessment tools have been developed to assess contextual issues, the tools that appear to provide the best information for youth at risk of academic failure and underachievement are the School Success Profile (SSP) and the Elementary School Success Profile (ESSP). The SSP, developed by Bowen and Richman (2001), is a survey questionnaire with 220 multiple choice items designed to help school practitioners assess middle school and high school students' perceptions of neighborhood, school, peer, and family conditions. The SSP contains no questions about illegal behavior, substance abuse, sexual activities, or issues of child abuse that may place youth or families in self-incriminating situations (Richman et al., 2004, p. 152). Validity and reliability measures of the SSP have been empirically supported across a number of research intervention studies (Bowen & Bowen, 1999; Bowen, Woolley, Richman, & Bowen, 2001; Nash, 2002). The ESSP also includes input from parents and teachers (Richman et al., 2004). The ESSP assesses neighborhood conditions, school environment, friend networks, family relationships, parent education involvement, child well-being, social behavior at home and school, and school performance. Like the SSP, the ESSP has demonstrated good reliability and validity in national studies. The SSP and ESSP assessment tools can assist the school practitioner in developing appropriate family, peer, school, and neighborhood interventions for individual youth and will help in monitoring change over time.

### Individual, Parent, and Schoolwide Interventions

Research supports the use of cognitive-behavioral interventions in assisting individual children experiencing underachievement or academic failure in building resiliency by increasing problem-solving skills, promoting prosocial peer connections, and increasing social competence (Friedberg & McClure, 2002; Stallard, 2002). Cognitive-behavioral treatment (CBT) uses a collaborative model, is time limited, focuses on the here and now, and promotes a skill-based learning approach. The empirical support for CBT for children and youth with externalizing conditions, anxiety, and depression is relatively strong (Weisz & Jensen, 1999). The results of randomized trials of CBT suggest that CBT fits into the category of "probably efficacious" interventions based on the framework developed by the American Psychological Association (Lonigan, Elbert, & Johnson, 1998). This category requires having two or more CBT studies that demonstrate superiority in outcomes when compared to wait-listed children. Cognitive-behavioral interventions help children learn to identify feelings and thoughts, to connect feelings and thoughts, and to change thoughts. Cognitive-behavioral interventions work best with children of at least 7 years of age (Kazdin, 2003).

## Tools and Practice Examples

Key steps for school practitioners in using CBT for children 7 years or older who are experiencing underachievement and academic failure are identified by Stallard (2002). These include

1. developing a clear and shared understanding of the relationship between how students think, how they feel, and what they do;
2. engaging in thought monitoring, which helps students to focus on core beliefs about their situation, their negative automatic thoughts, and situations that produce overly negative or self-critical thoughts;

3. identifying common negative thoughts or assumptions;
4. testing and evaluating these assumptions and helping the student engage in balanced thinking or cognitive restructuring;
5. teaching new cognitive skills that promote positive self-talk, consequential thinking, and problem solving;
6. addressing emotional education through monitoring and managing core emotions by teaching relaxation training and other preventive strategies;
7. managing reinforcers, practicing tasks, testing predictions, doing homework assignments; and
8. role-playing, modeling, and rehearsal.

Throughout the intervention process, the school practitioner needs to establish reinforcements and rewards that address the student's commitment to the intervention process. The reinforcements and rewards may be through contingency contracts, student self-reinforcements, or plans based on performance.

The use of worksheets that address each CBT step and the use of related homework help engage students in CBT. Helping students tune into their feelings might involve using puppets, feelings charts, games, or sentence completion exercises that focus on what happens when the child feels sad, angry, upset, excited, unhappy, or disappointed. Use of metaphors like a volcano erupting or a balloon bursting may help students monitor the depth of their feelings. To help students link thoughts and feelings, students may complete a situation, thoughts, and feelings chart. Using this chart, students would record the day and time, what happened (the situation), their thoughts about what happened, and the feelings that they had when the situation occurred. To help students engage in balanced thinking or cognitive restructuring, school practitioners can use thought thermometers (ranging from 1 = don't believe at all to 10 = very strongly believe) or worksheets that have students record the day and time, what their thoughts were, what evidence there was to support these thoughts, what evidence challenges these thoughts, and what would be more balanced thoughts (Friedberg & McClure, 2002; Stallard, 2002). For children and youth experiencing underachievement or academic failure, recording their thoughts when they are studying, taking tests, or answering questions in class may be the first step in changing the way students engage in school. When asked to do schoolwork by teachers or parents, students who are experiencing academic problems may have trigger thoughts like "I know I can't do this" or "I don't know what to do" or "I'm sure I will do this wrong." Another way for students to track movement toward balanced thinking is have them respond to the following questions developed by Stallard (2002, pp. 79–80):

1. What evidence is there to support this thought?
2. What evidence is there to question this thought?

3. What would my best friend/teacher/parent say if he or she heard me thinking in this way?
4. What would I say to my best friend if he or she had this thought?
5. Am I making any thinking errors?
6. Am I having a downer on myself and forgetting my strengths?
7. Am I blowing things up (all-or-nothing thinking, magnifying the negative, or snowballing?
8. Am I predicting failure?
9. Are these feeling thoughts?
10. Am I setting myself up to fail?
11. Am I blaming myself for the things that have gone wrong?

Teaching problem-solving skills as part of CBT helps children and youth approach challenging academic situations by developing effective solutions. Kazdin (2003) developed an interpersonal cognitive problem-solving skills training program (PSST) that consists of 12–20 weekly individual sessions, each of which usually lasts 30–50 minutes. The first few sessions focus on teaching the child the steps involved in problem solving; the next sessions use role-plays and games to help the child or youth practice the problem-solving steps; the remaining sessions focus on using problem-solving skills in real-life situations. Parents are involved in the middle phase of the intervention and are taught the problem-solving steps so that they can reinforce the skills in the home environment. To help children and youth operationalize the problem-solving steps, Kazdin (2003, p. 246) developed a series of self-statement steps to solve a problem. These self-statements steps are the following:

1. I must understand what I am supposed to do.
2. I have to look at all the possibilities.
3. I'd better concentrate and focus.
4. I need to make a choice.
5. I did a good job (or) Oh, I made a mistake.

Methods that help children to control their feelings include relaxing through controlled breathing (slowly drawing in the breath, holding it for 5 seconds, then slowly letting it out); engaging in physical exercise (e.g., walking briskly, jumping rope, running); and using progressive muscle relaxation methods (tensing muscles for 3 to 5 seconds).

While most children and youth benefit from CBT in schools, strong home–school collaboration appears to be particularly important for families of children and youth who are experiencing academic failure and are living in socially or economically disadvantaged communities (Raffaele & Knoff, 1999). Research indicates that effective school–home collaborations need to be proactive, sensitive to and respectful of the cultural backgrounds of students and families, and attentive to parental contributions to the educational process (Raffaele & Knoff, 1999). One model of this collaboration that has demonstrated positive outcomes for children is the Conjoint Behavioral Consultation (CBC) model. The CBC model is defined as "a structured, indirect form of service-delivery, in which parents and teachers are joined to work together to address academic, social or behavioral needs of an individual for whom both parties bear some responsibility" (Sheridan & Kratochwill, 1992, p. 122). Parents and teachers engage in a structured problem-solving process with a school practitioner to collaboratively address the needs of children at home and at school (Sheridan, Eagle, Cowan, & Mickelson, 2001).

The CBC steps involve (1) conjoint problem identification; (2) conjoint problem analysis; (3) treatment implementation; and (4) conjoint treatment evaluation (Sheridan et al., 2001). In the first step, school practitioners help parents and teachers identify the child's needs at home and at school. The parents and teachers decide on target behaviors for intervention. The school practitioner helps parents and teachers develop procedures for collecting baseline data on the target behaviors. These procedures might include keeping a daily record of particular behaviors, noting when the child is on task, or monitoring the parents' or teacher's reactions to the child's behavior. In the second step, parents and teachers evaluate the baseline data, decide on behavioral goals for the child, and discuss conditions that might help the child reach—or deter the child from—the target behaviors (Sheridan et al., 2001). During the third step, treatment implementation, the school practitioner reinforces and supports parent and teacher intervention efforts. In the final step, parents and teachers evaluate the effectiveness of the interventions and determine if further consultation is needed.

The goals of CBC are to establish partnerships between parents and teachers that will benefit the student and to develop and enhance the skills and competencies of parents and teachers in meeting the student's needs. Studies have supported the use of CBC for children at risk for underachievement and academic failure, especially for elementary and middle school children (Sheridan et al., 2001).

While individual and parental interventions are critical to helping students who are underachieving or failing academically, a more preventive, schoolwide intervention is needed to promote school success for all students. Several federal and community initiatives have developed prevention programs, both universal and targeted, that promote positive behavioral supports in the schools and academic success. One model of a schoolwide program that has demonstrated positive outcomes is Project ACHIEVE.

Project ACHIEVE, which has been implemented in schools and school districts across the country since 1990, is a comprehensive approach to maximizing children's academic, social, emotional, and behavioral progress (Knoff, Finch, & Carlyon, 2004). Through Project ACHIEVE, all regular education teachers, special education teachers, and support staff learn how to assess and address academic and behavioral problems (Hoagwood & Johnson, 2003).

According to Knoff et al. (2004, p. 19-6), Project ACHIEVE has six primary goals: (1) to enhance the problem-solving skills of teachers and other educators; (2) to improve the classroom and behavior-management skills of school personnel and the prosocial and self-management skills of students; (3) to ensure a high-quality education to all students in the school and to intervene strategically with students who are not performing at acceptable levels; (4) to aid the social and academic progress of students by strengthening the commitment of parents and community; (5) to validate the school's comprehensive improvement process; and (6) to create a school culture in which every teacher, staff member, and parent believes that everyone is responsible for every student. Schools that have implemented Project ACHIEVE experienced declines in special education referrals, disciplining referrals, and out-of-school suspensions; they also saw improvements in student achievement in comparison to a demographically matched sample (Hoagwood & Johnson, 2003; Knoff et al., 2004).

Three of the components of Project ACHIEVE are especially useful for school practitioners: (1) behavioral consultations and interventions; (2) referral question consultation (RQC); and (3) parent training, tutoring, and support. A critical component of the behavioral consultation and intervention component involves instruction of prosocial skills using social learning theory principles that are sensitive to cultural diversity (Cartledge & Milburn, 1996). The Stop and Think Social Skills Program (Knoff, 2001) for elementary and middle school students is an example of a social learning approach that teaches students more than 60 behavioral skills that are designed to motivate them and engage them academically. The 60 skills can be organized into four areas: survival skills (e.g., listening, following directions); interpersonal skills (e.g., sharing, waiting your turn, asking for permission); problem-solving skills (e.g., asking for help, deciding what to do, accepting consequences); and conflict resolution skills (e.g., dealing with teasing, losing, peer pressure). Five problem-solving steps are taught and reinforced: (1) Stop and think! (2) Are you going to make a good choice or bad choice? (3) What are your choices or steps? (4) Do it! and (5) Good job! (Knoff, 2001). The RQC component uses a systematic, problem-solving approach that shifts school practice from refer-test-place to one that fosters consultation and classroom-based interventions when problems surface (Knoff et al., 2004). This promotes linking assessment and intervention to student success and progress. The parent training, tutoring, and support component focuses on training parents to transfer the social skills and discipline/behavior management approaches of the school into the home and teaching them how to monitor their child's homework and academic achievement. Space in the school is dedicated to drop-in centers for parents in an effort to increase their participation in the school.

Promoting school success requires more than one level of intervention by school practitioners. Maintaining a school culture that fosters safety, caring, and positive adult involvement (parents, teachers, and staff) in the lives of students requires that schools address the challenges and risk conditions that children encounter, whether from themselves or their peers, their families, their schools, or their neighborhoods. School practitioners need to promote conditions that build resiliency and school success especially for children who are doing poorly in school.

More information on the SSP and the ESSP is available at http://www.schoolsuccessprofile.org. Information on the Stop and Think Social Skills Program is available from the National Mental Health and Education Center at http://www.naspcenter.org

## Key Points to Remember

- Children who are underachieving or failing at school can benefit from individual, parent, and schoolwide interventions that build resiliency and promote school success.
- Using an ecologically based resiliency framework for understanding the complex factors that place children and youth at risk for underachievement or academic failure will help school practitioners to assess what type of interventions can best help these children and youth.
- In assessing the causes for underachievement and academic failure, school practitioners need to take into account the child's intellectual abilities and contextual factors (at school, in the family, with peers, and in the neighborhood).
- CBT helps children learn how to identify their feelings and thoughts, how to connect feelings and thoughts, and how to change thoughts. CBT uses a collaborative model, is time limited, focuses on the here and now, and promotes skill-based learning.
- School-home collaborations join parents and teachers as partners in developing interventions that target problem behaviors. The CBC model is one example of a collaboration that shows promise for children who are underachieving or failing in school.
- To prevent academic failure, schoolwide intervention approaches that promote school success for all students need to be implemented. Schoolwide approaches such as Project ACHIEVE offer universal and targeted interventions.

# 3

## Guides for Designing and Establishing Alternative School Programs for Dropout Prevention

*David R. Dupper*

## Getting Started

The purpose of this chapter is to describe best practices in designing and establishing alternative education schools and programs for students who are at risk of dropping out of school as a result of truancy, poor grades, disruptive behavior, pregnancy, repeated suspensions, or expulsions. Following a brief overview of the history of alternative education in the United States and two opposing models of alternative education, this chapter discusses those best practices, based on empirical research, that are common across successful alternative education programs. It also discusses several obstacles or challenges that may arise in implementing these best practices and provides a series of steps to build a broad base of support for alternative education programs and services as well as assist in overcoming or reducing obstacles and barriers. This is followed by a case illustration that shows how a number of the best practices discussed in this chapter have been used in an alternative school in Idaho. The chapter concludes with several important points to remember and additional resources that can be used by school social workers and other student-service professionals interested in designing and establishing alternative education schools and programs.

### Alternative Education in the United States

The alternative school movement began in earnest in the 1960s as a response to the failure of traditional schools to address the needs of large groups of students (Kershaw & Blank, 1993; Raywid, 1990, 1994). The mission of these early alternative schools was to reach students who were unsuccessful in traditional school settings or disaffected with schooling and provide them with an opportunity to learn in a different academic setting (Ascher, 1982; Atkins, Allen, & Meredith, n.d.; Gregg, 1998).

Over the last decade, public concerns with violence, weapons, and drugs have led to a dramatic shift from an educational purpose to a disciplinary or correctional purpose in alternative education (Gregg, 1998). For example, alternative schools today are often viewed as places where disruptive, deviant, and dysfunctional students are sent "in order to protect and benefit the students who remain in traditional schools" (McGee, 2001, p. 589). Rather than focusing on fixing the educational environment, today's public alternative schools focus on fixing the student and keeping "problem kids" out of our regular schools and off the street. See Table 3.1 for a comparison of these two opposing models of alternative education in relation to school climate (culture), staffing issues, curriculum and instruction, and entrance and exit criteria.

**Table 3.1** Educational Versus Disciplinary Models of Alternative Education

|  | Educational (fix the educational environment) | Disciplinary (fix the child) |
| --- | --- | --- |
| Climate | • Challenging, caring, nurturing, supportive<br>• Collaborative<br>• Student-centered<br>• Personal relationships, bonding to faculty and other students<br>• Focus on whole child<br>• High expectations for student achievement, behavior<br>• Student behavior guided by norms | • Controlling<br>• Highly structured, regulated<br>• Student compliance<br>• Student behavior controlled by rules<br>• Focus on behavior<br>• Punitive |
| Staffing | • Teacher chooses, not assigned<br>• Hiring, seniority waivers may be needed<br>• May be contracted on part-time or as-needed basis to meet graduation, IEP requirements<br>• Teacher assumes multiple roles (teacher, mentor, counselor)<br>• Repertoire of teaching skills, strategies<br>• Caring, humane<br>• Accountable for student success<br>• Collegiality, teamwork<br>• Professional community | • Controlling<br>• Highly structured, regulated<br>• Student compliance<br>• Student behavior controlled by rules<br>• Focus on behavior<br>• Punitive |
| Curriculum and instruction | • Full instructional program<br>• Integrated curriculum, interdisciplinary projects<br>• Individualized (for learning styles, needs, current achievement levels)<br>• Clear program goals<br>• Experiential, hands-on learning<br>• Vocational, career, community service components | • Academics not the focus<br>• Provides only basics, no electives<br>• Skill and drill<br>• Lessons may be provided by home school |

*(continued)*

| | Educational (fix the educational environment) | Disciplinary (fix the child) |
|---|---|---|
| **Table 3.1** *(Continued)* | | |
| | • Challenging, engaging, relevant<br>• Structured for early, frequent success<br>• Continuous progress model<br>• Student responsibility for learning<br>• Multidisciplinary: academic, behavioral, social contexts | • Behavior modification<br>• Remediation |
| Entrance/ exit criteria | • Students attend by choice<br>• Long-term; students may graduate from program | • Student assigned or given limited<br>• options (e.g., alternative school or jail)<br>• Short-term (1 day, rest of semester, rest of year); student returns to host school when time or behavior requirements met<br>• By contract with parent, child<br>• Transition services critical<br>• Collaboration with home school, support system for returning students important |

*Source*: Adapted from Appalachia Educational Laboratory. (1998). *Schools for disruptive students: A questionable alternative?* Policy Briefs Series. Charleston, WV: Author. Reprinted with permission.

As seen in Table 3.1, alternative schools with an educational focus ("fix the environment") are student-centered, caring, humane learning environments where personal relationships are emphasized and the curriculum is delivered experientially. These alternative schools are more long-term in nature because they focus on the transition from school to work through vocational training (Atkins et al., n.d.). On the other hand, alternative schools with a disciplinary focus ("fix the child") are highly structured, punitive environments where student compliance is emphasized and behavior modification rather than academics is emphasized. These alternative schools and programs are more short-term in nature, and they focus on improving students' behavior and returning them to their home schools (Atkins et al., n.d.). It is important to note that researchers have found that alternative schools that are correctional in nature, focusing on punitive disciplinary policies and practices, "reap no positive long-term gains and may even increase negative outcomes" (Gregg, 1998, p. 3). On the other hand, alternative schools that focus on education rather than punishment work best in improving student behavior and student achievement (Kershaw & Blank, 1993; Morley, 1991; Raywid, 1994). Research also shows that alternative schools and programs that focus primarily on therapeutic interventions may "temporarily improve student behavior and achievement[,] but results tend to fade when students return to home schools" (Gregg, 1998, p. 5).

## What We Know

### Empirically Supported Characteristics Common to Successful Alternative Education Programs

One of the most comprehensive definitions of today's alternative school is provided by the U.S. Department of Education. It defines an alternative school as "a public elementary/secondary school that addresses needs of students that typically cannot be met in a regular school, provides nontraditional education, serves as an adjunct to a regular school, or falls outside the categories of regular, special education, or vocational education (U.S. Department of Education, 2002, p. 55). Daniel Wiltrout, a consultant with the Wisconsin Department of Instruction, defines alternative schools as schools in a different setting that offer flexible schedules, smaller teacher–student ratios, and modified curriculum to serve students not succeeding in traditional public school environments (National Conference of State Legislatures, 2004). Rather than providing a definition, Morley (1991, p. 8) describes alternative education as "a perspective, not a procedure or program. It is based upon the belief that there are many ways to become educated, as well as many types of environments and structures within which this may occur." This viewpoint assumes that all children do not learn in the same manner and that the core of alternative education lies in varied methods of instruction and an innovative curriculum (Reimer & Cash, 2003).

   Though it is possible to provide definitions and philosophical perspectives about alternative education, it is much more difficult to discuss the effectiveness of alternative schools and programs, largely because so few rigorous studies have been done in this area (Lange & Sletten, 2002). In one of the few studies to date, Cox, Davidson, and Bynum (1995) used meta-analysis to summarize empirical research on alternative schools in the years 1966–1993. Their final meta-analysis included 57 evaluations of alternative schools that met the following criteria: the program being evaluated consisted of a separate curriculum, was housed outside a conventional school, and statistically assessed at least one type of outcome (e.g., student attitudes toward school, school performance, self-esteem, delinquency). Based on their meta-analysis, these authors found that

- alternative schools targeting a specific population (primarily low achievers or delinquents) have more impact than programs not targeting specific types of students;
- alternative schools have small positive effects on attitudes and performance outcomes;
- however, these authors also found that alternative schools do not affect delinquent behavior; that is, their effect on school performance and self-esteem is not large enough to influence delinquent behavior.

In a recent publication, Reimer and Cash (2003) have analyzed a number of empirical studies by researchers in alternative education (Kadel, 1994; Kellmayer, 1995; Public Schools of North Carolina, 2000; Raywid, 1994; Schargel & Smink, 2001; Wehlage, 1983) and contributed to the knowledge base by identifying a number of characteristics and best practices of successful alternative schools. A number of other researchers (Ascher, 1982; Barr & Parrett, 2001; Chavkin, 1993; Cox et al., 1995; Dollar, 1983; Franklin & Streeter, 1991; Ingersoll & LeBoeuf, 1997; Kraemer & Ruzzi, 2001; Morley, 1991; Northwest Regional Educational Laboratory, 2001; U.S. Department of Education, 1996; Young, 1990) have also contributed to our understanding of characteristics that distinguish successful alternative programs from unsuccessful programs.

Table 3.2 contains a comprehensive list of characteristics and best practices common to successful alternative programs based on the empirical research. Research indicates that perhaps the single most important characteristic in developing an alternative school or program is employing teachers and staff who have chosen to work with and are committed to these youth. The selection of committed and caring staff is of paramount importance because "students can overcome bad teaching but they may never recover from a bad teacher who fails to project a true sense of caring and concern" (Reimer & Cash, 2003, p. 19). Successful alternative programs provide ongoing staff development in the areas of classroom management techniques, diversity training, and alternative instructional methods because most teachers did not receive this training in their formal teacher education program (Reimer & Cash, 2003). It also appears that successful alternative programs target a specific population of at-risk students and develop a holistic, humane, flexible educational program that is individualized and responsive to the social, emotional, and academic needs of these youth. Meeting the academic needs of these youth requires a hands-on, experiential curriculum that is tailored to the unique learning style of each student. Unfortunately, there is little or no data related to what happens to alternative school graduates upon reentry into their home school. However, there is evidence to suggest that long-term outcomes may be enhanced by providing follow-up and transition services to these students (Atkins et al., n.d; Glass, 1995).

**Table 3.2** Characteristics and Best Practices Common to Successful Alternative Education Programs

- A student-to-staff ratio that is lower than in mainstream schools (i.e., maximum teacher/student ratio of 1:10) (Ingersoll & LeBoeuf, 1997; Northwest Regional Educational Laboratory, 2001; Schargel & Smink, 2001)
- Small student base not exceeding 250 students (Schargel & Smink, 2001)
- A clear stated mission shared by all staff and clear rules that are enforced fairly and consistently (Cox, Davidson, & Bynum, 1995; Ingersoll & LeBoeuf, 1997; Northwest Regional Educational Laboratory, 2001; Schargel & Smink, 2001)
- A caring faculty who have chosen to teach in alternative schools and programs and who are committed to counseling, mentoring, and tutoring students in these programs (Barr & Parrett, 2001; Northwest Regional Educational Laboratory, 2001; Schargel & Smink, 2001)
- Continual staff development opportunities (Schargel & Smink, 2001)
- School staff having high academic standards and high expectations for student achievement (Schargel & Smink, 2001)
- Focus is on individualized learning that takes into account student's expectations and learning style within a flexible schedule that allows students to work at their own pace (Ascher, 1982; Chavkin, 1993; Dollar, 1983; Franklin & Streeter, 1991; Northwest Regional Educational Laboratory, 2001; Schargel & Smink, 2001)
- One-on-one interaction between teachers and students with a total commitment to have each student be successful (Morley, 1991; Schargel & Smink, 2001; Young, 1990)
- A school or program that targets specific populations (i.e., primarily low school achievers or delinquents) (Chavkin, 1993; Cox, Davidson, & Bynum, 1995; Franklin & Streeter, 1991)
- Strong stable, and dynamic leadership (Reimer & Cash, 2003)
- Provide a supportive, informal setting where personal relationships between students and teachers and a "family-like atmosphere" of respect can flourish (Morley, 1991; Northwest Regional Educational Laboratory, 2001; Schargel & Smink, 2001; Young 1990)
- Provide a curriculum that can be described as "applied," "experiential," "hands-on," or "integrated"; a curriculum that emphasizes "real life learning" and that makes connections between the school and the community or "work world" (Ingersoll & LeBoeuf, 1997; Kraemer & Ruzzi, 2001; Northwest Regional Educational Laboratory, 2001; Reimer & Cash, 2003; Young, 1990)

*(continued)*

**Table 3.2** *(Continued)*

- Holistic services are provided to meet the emotional, physical, and academic needs of students (Reimer & Cash, 2003)
- Student voices in decision-making and school operations is emphasized (Ascher, 1982; Morley, 1991; Northwest Regional Educational Laboratory, 2001; Young 1990)
- Broad participation of the family and community is emphasized (Ascher, 1982; Chavkin, 1993; Franklin & Streeter, 1991; Ingersoll & LeBoeuf, 1997; Reimer & Cash, 2003)
- Strong working relations with all parts of the school system and with other collaborating agencies that provide critical services to youth (Northwest Regional Educational Laboratory, 2001)

# What We Can Do

## Steps in Designing and Establishing Effective Alternative Education Schools and Programs

The recent emphasis on zero tolerance and punitive discipline as a response to student misbehavior poses a number of significant challenges for school social workers and other student service professionals in designing and establishing effective alternative schools and programs. With a general public clamoring for punishment and making "bad kids" pay for their school misbehavior and poor attitude, many alternative schools have evolved into dumping grounds to warehouse children. A central challenge awaiting school social workers and others is to convince the general public, as well as some teachers and administrators, that effective and humane alternative programs must offer students opportunities to learn from their mistakes and move forward positively with their lives, rather than focusing exclusively on punishment. School social workers and counselors must be prepared to challenge comments and attitudes such as the following one made by a school superintendent in North Carolina: "I'm not going to waste my certified teachers on those kids" (North Carolina Education and Law Project, 1997, p. 3).

To overcome obstacles such as these, it is essential that school social workers and others plan and implement in a carefully thought out and systematic manner. The following series of sequential steps are based on the work of Reimer and Cash (2003), DeBlois (1994), Dugger and DesMoulin-Kherat (1996), and Harrington-Lueker (1994). They are designed to build a broad base of support in the initial phases of program development, to help overcome potential barriers and obstacles throughout the process, and to ensure that programs are built upon those characteristics and best practices outlined in Table 3.2.

1. *Establish a planning team or task force.* To ensure a broad base of support, it is recommended that this planning team or task force include representatives of local social service agencies, local businesses, law enforcement, and schools. It will work best if it has 6 to 15 members. Reimer and Cash (2003) state that teams with more than 15 members "become cumbersome to work with and may become splintered as time goes on. Conversely, a subgroup or a powerful leader who wants to push through his/her own vision and agenda may sway a small group" (p. 17). It is advisable to start putting the team together at least 1 year ahead of the start-up date of a school or program. See Dupper (1993) for a detailed discussion of a community task force that was an integral part of an alternative program for potential dropouts in a middle school setting.

2. *Develop a philosophy and mission for the school or program.* A group consensus on the philosophical foundation is absolutely essential since this will guide the development of program policies and procedures (Reimer & Cash, 2003). A central question is whether the school or program is envisioned as educational (focused on providing an alternative learning experience) or disciplinary (focused on "fixing the child"). These two opposing philosophies are described and contrasted in Table 3.1. In determining which of these philosophies will be chosen, it is essential that school social workers and counselors make the planning team or task force aware of current research on characteristics and best practices of alternative programs (see Table 3.2).

3. *Develop the design and operation of the school or program.* This is the point at which a building principal or program director should be hired to decide on the nuts and bolts of the school or program with advice from school district staff. At this stage of the process it is important to consider how the school or program will receive funding (per-student costs for alternative education are higher because of the lower teacher–student ratio), where it will be located (i.e., settings for alternative schools and programs range from space in a large department store to an empty office building to a portable structure), how large it will be, whom it will serve, how transportation will be provided, and how it will be staffed. Again, it is essential that the school social worker and counselors share best practices related to each of these issues. At this point, it is also important to remember that applying for grants and holding annual fund-raising events is time consuming and tiresome (DeBlois, 1994). If the school district is too small or lacks the financial resources to support an alternative school, look into participating in a regional program run by an education service district (Northwest

Regional Educational Laboratory, 2001). However, if one of the goals of the program is for students to reenter their traditional or base school, then it may be helpful to be located in or near that school. It is essential that good two-way communication between the alternative and students' home schools be maintained, particularly as students are preparing to transition back to their home schools (Reimer & Cash, 2003).

4. *Select staff members.* Because of the deep suspicion and distrust that many students feel toward a school system that they believe has failed them, it is extremely important that a fragile bond of two-way trust between students and staff be established (Kraemer & Ruzzi, 2001). This is particularly true if students will be assigned to the alternative school or program rather than attend by choice. Since many of these youth have difficulty following traditional school rules, it is important that the principal or administrator in charge of student discipline also be flexible in dealing with discipline issues (Reimer & Cash, 2003).

5. *Design the alternative curriculum.* In this step, the planning team or task force must decide upon the teacher–student ratio, what curriculum will be offered, how the curriculum will be delivered, how technology will be integrated, how social services and counseling services will be delivered, and how to provide opportunities for teachers to collaborate and plan together. It should be emphasized that the most important role of each and every staff member is to be an *informal counselor and support person to students* (Kellmayer, 1995).

6. *Build community support.* One of the most effective ways of changing the public's negative perception of alternative education is by "inviting community members, including the local press, to visit your alternative school as well as to be able to document the ways in which students have grown while attending the alternative school" (McGee, 2001, p. 589). It is important to connect with surrounding businesses and community groups for ways that they can become involved (e.g., providing money and career-related opportunities). When possible, involve parents and family, particularly at the middle school level, by, for example, sending letters to them and holding parenting classes and student-led parent conferences.

7. *Establish specific enrollment and exit criteria.* Enrollment criteria must be established to prevent the alternative school or program from becoming a place where the school district dumps students who don't seem to fit anywhere else. "If the school or program becomes a dumping ground for students it was not intended to serve, it is likely that the once-enthusiastic staff will become frustrated and begin to leave the school. These teachers may be replaced with others who do not share the original vision of the

school, thus causing the program's reputation to suffer and enrollment to decline" (Northwest Regional Educational Laboratory, 2001).

8. *Document and publicize program results.* To avoid closure because of school board changes, opposition from teacher's unions (Amenta, 1997), or an economic downturn (DeBlois, 1994), alternative school administrators and staff must constantly sell their program by showing that it works and that it is cost effective e.g., it is cheaper to educate now than to build prisons later). This can be accomplished through statistics, anecdotes, and personal testimony from students and parents. To assess improvements in learning, data on changes in GPA, attendance rates, graduation rates, and dropout rates should be collected and analyzed over several years (Gregg, 1998). To assess improvements in student behavior, data on changes in the number of disciplinary referrals, suspension or expulsion rates, and in-school suspension rates should be collected and analyzed over several years (Gregg, 1998).

# Tools and Practice Examples

## A Case Illustration

The following is excerpted from an article titled "Where Everyone Knows Your Name! Special Programs Target at-Risk Students" from the publication *Education World* (1998). It describes Meridian Academy alternative high school in Meridian, Idaho, a suburb of Boise. It provides an example of how the best practices discussed in this article have been applied in an alternative school.

> All the teachers were glad to have me. They make [me] feel important—as a person. It blew my mind. I loved it from the first day. Everybody is really welcoming.—John, a tenth-grade dropout from a large high school
>
> There were too many kids there. I sat in the back and raised my hand, but I never got any help.... Here, everyone is very accepting. I know I'm going to graduate.—Anna, who failed her freshman year in a big high school

The 150-student academy is a good example of an alternative high school that incorporates a number of the characteristics and best practices contained in Table 3.2. It is described as a school where "invisible" children who got lost in the shuffle of larger schools are offered a new chance for success. Students attend small classes (15 in the average class) where teachers greet them by name every day; where teachers strive to draw every student into every lesson, engaging the students and making them feel "visible"; and where small "family group" sessions offer students an opportunity to air problems and receive support on a regular basis. The curriculum at Meridian is hands-on and student centered. Instead of reading out of a book and answering the questions in the back, students become involved by building it, or making it, or doing it. Meridian has a no-homework policy. Meridian staff recognize that many at-risk students fall behind because they can't keep up with the homework assigned in regular schools. Many come from home situations that are not conducive to doing homework, and many have after-school jobs, parenting responsibilities, or go to vocational school at night. To compensate, class time is extended, and Friday afternoons are dedicated to finishing or making up work. As an added incentive to staying on top of work, students who are caught up with their work get to leave early on Fridays. Discipline is not much of a problem at Meridian Academy. The staff and even the students recognize that structure is a key to success: lack of structure at home and in school are some of the main causes for the students' previous school problems. Each student must sign the school's student behavior policy each semester. It's a policy that the students have a hand in forming, and it spells out school rules and consequences. After three discipline referrals, students must appear before a student court where evidence is presented and students and parents have an opportunity to make their pleas. Staff members then vote to give the students another chance or to dismiss them. Academic expectations are very high. Students must achieve a 70% record in each class. Each year, 75% of students complete the school year. One teacher comments, "It only takes a few weeks and you notice they raise their heads up. Next they start looking you in the eye, and their shoulders are back. Pretty soon, they start thinking about vocational school, or technical school or college—the last thing they ever thought about in their lives."

## Resources

Dupper, D. R. (1993). School–community collaboration: A description of a model program designed to prevent school dropouts. *School Social Work Journal, 18*, 32–39. (This article provides a detailed discussion of a community task force and its importance in the overall operation of an alternative program.)

Northwest Regional Educational Laboratory, Alternative schools: Caring for kids on the edge, *Northwest Education Magazine* (summer 1998). This organization can be reached at 101 S.W. Main Street, Suite 500, Portland, OR 97204, Telephone (503) 275-9500, e-mail: webmaster@nwrel.org, NWREL Web Site: http://www.nwrel.org

The Center for Effective Collaboration and Practice. *Alternative schools: Information for families.* Available at http://cecp.air.org/familybriefs/docs/AltSch.pdf

The National Dropout Prevention Center (NDPC) at Clemson University has become a well-established national resource for sharing solutions for student success. The center can be reached at 209 Martin Street, Clemson, SC 29631-1555 (864) 656-2599, e-mail: ndpc@ clemson.edu; http://www.dropoutprevention.org/

National Coalition of Advocates for Students is a private nonprofit coalition of advocacy organizations that work on behalf of students who are traditionally underserved (e.g., students of color, immigrants, students from low-income families, and special needs students). E-mail: ncasmfe@aol.com; Web Site: http://www.ncas1.org/

*Quality alternative placements for suspended or expelled students: "Lessons learned" from the Center for the Prevention of School Violence's Youth Out of the Education Mainstream Initiative* can be downloaded at http://www.ncdjjdp.org/cpsv/ alt_learning/yoem/qareplace.htm

Kennedy, R. L., & Morton, J. H. (1999). *A school for healing: Alternative strategies for teaching at-risk students.* New York: Peter Lang.

For state-by-state information on alternative schools for disruptive students, see http://www.ecs.org/clearinghouse/15/05/1505.htm. Successful alternative education programs for troubled youth can be downloaded from http://www. ncsl.org/programs/educ/AlterEdSN.htm

## Key Points to Remember

- A major challenge that school social workers and others face in designing and establishing effective and humane alternative schools and programs is to create schools and programs that are creative outlets for students whose needs are not being met by traditional schools. It is important to create places where students will have opportunities to learn from their mistakes and move forward positively with their lives rather than be warehoused as "bad kids."

- The ultimate outcome for the majority of students in an alternative school or program is a successful reentry into their base school. Therefore, ongoing communication with the base school is essential, and adequate supports (e.g., transition specialists) must be provided to the students as they reenter. Evidence suggests that providing follow-up and transition services to students as they return to their home schools may enhance long-term outcomes.

- Target specific populations of at-risk students (e.g., low achievers or delinquents). Targeted programs have been shown to be more effective than programs that do not target specific types of students.

- Plan for the maximum level of voluntary participation by both students and teachers. Hire teachers with both the skills and the passion to teach material in an experiential, creative, and noncompetitive manner. Develop an organizational structure characterized by flexibility and autonomy, one in which students, teachers, and parents can work together to make program decisions.

- Follow the eight steps described in this chapter focusing on the design and creation of effective alternative education schools and programs. Include as many of the characteristics contained in Table 3.2 as possible as these are, according to a number of researchers in the field of alternative education, the best practices.

# 4

# Solution-Focused, Brief Therapy Interventions for Students at Risk to Drop Out

*Cynthia Franklin*
*Johnny S. Kim*
*Stephen J. Tripodi*

## Getting Started

Youths from diverse cultures and backgrounds are currently dropping out of high school. The U.S. Department of Education's Institute of Education Sciences reports that high school dropout is a continuing problem for schools (What Works Clearinghouse, n.d., http://www.w-w-c.org/comingnext/dropout.html). The percentage of students who do not graduate from high school at the end of a 13-year program of study ranges from 11% to 28% for certain at-risk student populations. Some research suggests that high school dropouts are more likely to abuse drugs, be unemployed, and be in jail (Aloise-Young & Chavez, 2002). Every indication is that social, mental health, and family problems co-occur with high school dropout.

School social workers and other student support services professionals need effective interventions that can engage students and can develop a quick change in students' behaviors and attitudes. Since the 1990s, school social workers and counselors have been experimenting with solution-focused, brief therapy (SFBT) to assist students with academic and behavioral problems. SFBT developed out of family systems theory and social construction family practice. This chapter describes the steps in conducting SFBT and how it can be applied with students who are at risk of dropping out of high school.

## What We Know

Reasons for dropping out of high school often overlap in a way that makes it difficult to develop a singular profile of at-risk school dropouts. Reviews of this topic indicate that there are both institutional and individual reasons for dropouts (Rumberger, 2004). Table 4.1 provides a summary of individual-, family-, and school-related reasons for dropping out based on empirical studies.

It is easy to see when examining the reasons for dropping out of high school that, in order to prevent dropout, school social workers and other professionals need to be prepared to work with students across multiple problem issues and

**Table 4.1** Reasons for Dropping Out

| Individual | Family | School-Related |
|---|---|---|
| • Low grades<br>• Poor daily attendance<br>• Misbehavior<br>• Alcohol and drug use<br>• Feeling alienated from other students | • Parents not engaged in child's schooling<br>• Teen pregnancy<br>• Student getting married<br>• Financial and work reasons<br>• Permissive parenting style<br>• Negative emotional reactions and sanctions for bad grades | • Student/teacher ratio<br>• Quality of teachers<br>• Seeking smaller school size<br>• School safety concerns<br>• Not feeling welcomed at the school |

*Sources*: Based on studies by Aloise-Young & Chavez, 2002; Jordan, Lara, & McPartland, 1996; Rumberger, 1987; Rumberger, Ghatak, Poulos, Ritter, & Dornbusch, 1990; Rumberger & Thomas, 2000.

systems (e.g., school, family, and community). Yet, for all that has been written on preventing dropout, past reviews of research studies indicate that the research in this area is limited for the scope and importance of the problem (e.g., Prevatt & Kelly, 2003; Rumberger, 2004; Slavin & Fashola, 1998). Slavin and Fashola (1998), for example, reviewed the literature on dropout prevention programs and found only two programs that met evidence-based criteria for an effective intervention. Prevatt and Kelly (2003) conducted a thorough review of research evaluating dropout prevention programs and found that few studies have evaluated program effectiveness with strong designs and that schools are not adopting research-based prevention programs. The National Dropout Prevention Center (2004) lists 15 strategies for dropout prevention that have been found to have some degree of effectiveness (http://www.dropoutprevention.org/effstrat/effstrat. htm). Alternative school programs are one of the promising practices that are mentioned across reviews. See Chapter 3 for a discussion of how to design an effective alternative school program. The most comprehensive review on dropout prevention is Chad Nye and colleagues' study, sponsored by the What Works Clearinghouse (n.d., http://www.w-w-c.org/comingnext/dropout.html), a research arm of the Department of Education's Institute for Education Sciences. The What Works Clearinghouse (n.d.) uses a set of standards for evaluating studies on the basis of rigorous, experimental criteria. This group works in alliance with the Campbell Collaboration to synthesize the best practices in dropout prevention. Brian Cobb personal communication, May 27, 2005) and his colleagues at Colorado State University have also completed a large meta-analysis that includes approximately 50 dropout prevention programs for high-risk youths.

## Solution-Focused, Brief Therapy

SFBT originated in the early 1980s at the Brief Family Therapy Center in Milwaukee. This approach to counseling became very popular and widely used in the 1990s mostly because of the demands for briefer counseling interventions. Practitioners also began to use SFBT techniques in schools (Berg & Shilts, 2005; Franklin, Biever, Moore, Clemons, & Scamardo, 2001; Kral, 1995; Metcalf, 1995; Murphy, 1996; Sklare, 1997; Webb, 1999). As a result, quasi-experimental design studies began to examine the success of SFBT with students who have behavioral and academic problems. Table 4.2 presents examples of quasi-experimental studies that have been completed on SFBT in schools.

Even though studies on the effectiveness of SFBT with at-risk students are only in the infancy stage, this approach has shown some promise with challenging and resistant students. Franklin and Streeter (2003, 2005) focused their work on

**Table 4.2** Examples of Outcome Studies on Solution-Focused Therapy in Schools

*Posttest Only*

Author and Date: Littrell et al. (1995)
Population: Students (grades 9–12)
Sample Size: 61
Setting: High school
Number of Sessions: 3
Measures: Self-anchored scales
Results: No difference between brief therapy groups.

*Experimental or Quasi-Experimental Designs*

Author and Date: Franklin & Streeter (2005)
Population: High school dropout youths
Sample Size: 85
Setting: Alternative high school
Number of Sessions: Ongoing attendance at solution-focused high school program
Measures: School Success Profile, number of credits earned, attendance
Results: Results from the School Success Profile showed both the solution-focused group and comparison group are at high risk of dropping out with few assets or protective factors. The solution-focused group, however, rated school domain factors (school satisfaction, teacher support, school safety) as assets, while comparison group rated them as either caution or risk. The solution-focused group showed statistically significant differences on the credits earned, along with a moderate effect size. There was statistically significant difference on attendance favoring the comparison group, along with a large effect size. Authors report that the self-paced, instructional format of the solution-focused program may have confounded the attendance finding.

(*continued*)

**Table 4.2** *(Continued)*

Author and Date: Newsome (2004)
Population: Students
Sample Size: 52
Setting: Middle school
Number of Sessions: One class period (35 minutes) for 8 weeks
Measures: Grades and attendance
Results: Grades for students in the experimental group increased from a mean
pretest score of 1.58 to a mean posttest score of 1.69 while grades for
the comparison group decreased from a mean pretest score of 1.66 to
a posttest score of 1.48. The results of the regression testing differences
between experimental and comparison groups on posttest grade point
average scores was statistically significant when using pretest grade point
average as the covariate; however, the proportion of variance ($R^2$) was
not large. As for the other dependent variable, attendance, there was no
statistical difference between the experimental and comparison groups.

Author and Date: Moore & Franklin (2005)
Population: Students
Sample Size: 59
Setting: Middle school
Number of Sessions:
• 4-hour teacher training on solution model
• 3–4 teacher-therapist consultations
• 1–2 formal collaborative meetings between teachers and students
• 5–7 30–45-minute individual therapy sessions with students
Measures: Teacher Report Form of the Achenbach Behavioral Checklist, Youth
Self-Report of the Achenbach Behavioral Checklist
Results: Internalizing and externalizing scores for TRF showed that experimental
group declined below the clinical level by posttest and remained there
for follow-up. Comparison group changed little among pretest, posttest,
and follow-up. Effect size for internalizing was large while effect size
for externalizing was medium. Internalizing score for YSR showed no
difference between experimental and comparison groups, and effect
size was weak. Externalizing score for YSR showed the experimental
group dropped below the clinical level and continued to drop at
follow-up. A large effect size was calculated for YSR externalizing score.

Author and Date: LaFountain & Garner (1996)
Population: Students
Sample Size: 311
Setting: Elementary and high schools
Number of Sessions: 8
Measures: Index of Personality Characteristics
Results: Modest but statistically significant between-group differences were
found on three subscales of the Index of Personality Characteristics:
nonacademic, perception of self, and acting in. These differences

*(continued)*

**Table 4.2** *(Continued)*

suggest that students in the experimental group had higher self-esteem in nonacademic arenas; more positive attitudes and feelings about themselves; and more appropriate ways of coping with emotions.

Author and Date: Springer et al. (2000)
Population: Children
Sample Size: 10
Setting: School
Number of Sessions: 5
Measures: Hare Self-Esteem Scale
Results: Solution-focused subjects made significant pretest to posttest improvement on the Hare Self-Esteem Scale with a moderate effect size, whereas the comparison group's scores were unchanged. However, a covariance analysis of posttest scores (with pretest scores as the covariate) found no significant between-group differences. Limitations include small sample size and absence of randomization

*Single-Case and AB Designs*

Author and Date: Corcoran & Stephenson (2000)
Population: Children (most referred by schools)
Sample Size: 136
Setting: University-sponsored mental health clinic
Number of Sessions: 4–6
Measures: Feelings, Attitudes and Behaviors Scale for Children, Conners's Parent Rating Scale
Results: Results showed significant improvement from pretest to posttest for some subscales in the Conners's Parent Rating Scale: conduct problems, impulsivity, and hyperactivity.

Author and Date: Franklin et al. (2001)
Population: Learning-challenged middle-school students
Sample Size: 7
Setting: Middle school
Number of Sessions: 5–10
Measures: Conners's Teacher Rating Scale
Results: 5 of 7 (71 %) cases improved per teacher's report.

Author and Date: Geil (1998)
Population: Elementary-school children and teachers
Sample Size: 8 student–teacher pairs
Setting: Elementary school
Number of Sessions: 12 consultations
Measures: Instructional Environment System-II and Code for Instructional Structure and Student Academic Response
Results: Statistical difference in two of the consultation cases, only one solution-focused case.

using SFBT to prevent high school dropout. These researchers and practitioners focused on training teachers and administrators in solution-focused principles and techniques. The goal was to change the school culture so that all staff used a solution-building process with students at risk to drop out. These principles were developed in relationship to a study on dropout prevention.

SFBT practitioners believe that this counseling approach is effective in encouraging students to overcome personal and social barriers that are associated with dropping out of school. SFBT is helpful for adolescents at risk for dropping out because it focuses on moving students in crisis beyond their current state to a position of working through the crisis (Hopson & Kim, 2004). Students at risk for dropping out may have many different social problems or mental health or family issues. SFBT practitioners may address specific issues as barriers to student goals, but they do not try to solve all of these problems. Instead, the practitioners focus on the functional and social outcomes of these problems (e.g., tardiness, missing classes, conflicts with teachers) and help the students prioritize what needs most to be changed in their future behaviors so that they can get along with others (e.g., teacher, parents, peers, friends). The SFBT approach examines strengths in students and their social environment and seeks to harness those strengths to help them identify what is going to make a difference in their interactions. SFBT also may add resources to remove barriers that block goals and use whatever resources are available to help students succeed.

Solution-focused questioning techniques are used to build relationships with students, engage students in a solution-building process, discover their personal goals and strengths, and increase motivation toward desired outcomes. This chapter describes the solution-building process and the structure of a typical session and illustrates questioning techniques that may be useful with students who are at risk of dropping out.

## What Is Solution Building?

*Solution building* is a process where practitioners engage students in a purposeful conversation, resulting in changes in students' perceptions and social interactions. The solution-building process or conversation is often contrasted to the problem-solving process. Problem solving focuses on the resolution of presenting problems through understanding the problems, enumerating alternatives that can solve the problems, and choosing an alternative. In contrast, solution building changes the way people think about presenting problems and identifies future behaviors and tasks that have the potential to accomplish desired goals and outcomes (De Jong & Berg, 2002). Solution-building conversations result in the student discovering goals, tasks, and behaviors that change future outcomes. The SFBT practitioner acts as a catalyst or facilitator and creates an interpersonal context where solutions emerge from the students and their ideas during the process of conversation.

Change in SFBT comes from finding what already works and doing more of it (Miller & de Shazer, 2000). It also comes from helping students visualize a future outcome that they desire and helping them think through the steps to achieve it. The steps are further broken down into small tasks or solutions that are identified by the students. The reason why SFBT practitioners focus on small steps is to get students moving forward toward their goals and to help them be able to experience some success. Success builds confidence in students and has the potential to change their view of the situation (e.g., I was able to come back to school for one class with the teacher I like, so maybe I do not have to drop out). Small steps are also viewed as being capable of serving as catalysts for bigger changes.

## Solution-Focused, Brief Therapy Counseling Techniques
### Exception Questions
- When does the problem not occur?
- What was different about those times when things were better between you and your teacher?
- Even though this is a very bad time, in my experience, people's lives do not always stay the same. I will bet that there have been times when the problem of being sent to the principal's office was not happening, or at least was happening less. Please describe those times. What was different? How did you get that to happen?

SFBT practitioners start solution building by exploring exceptions (Lee, 1997). Exceptions are situations when the stated complaint does not occur, occurs less often, or occurs with less intensity. Exception questions were designed to encourage students to notice evidence that not only is change possible, but also that they have already had some successful attempts (Lathem, 2002). SFBT theorizes that it is more beneficial for students to increase their current successes instead of trying to eliminate the problem altogether, no matter how small the current successes appear to be (Murphy, 1996).

The school social worker and counselor must understand the students' perception of what has worked and what they think will work to achieve their goals, in addition to trusting the students in regard to seeing solutions in exceptions (Pichot & Dolan, 2003). It is important for the social worker and counselor to emphasize the exceptions and question how the student brought about these changes. Furthermore, the social worker must believe that it was not the right solution if the student walked away from it.

## Relationship Questions

- What would your teacher say about your grades?
- What would your mother say?
- If you were to do something that made your teacher very happy, what would that be?
- Who would be the most surprised if you did well on that test?

Relationship questions allow students to discuss their problems from a third-person point of view, which makes the problem less threatening and allows the social worker, counselor, or teacher to assess the students' viewpoint and the students to practice thinking about the problem from the viewpoint of others. The procedure is to ask the students what their family members and teachers think about their problem and progress, as more indicators of change help the students develop a vision of a future appropriate to their social context. Furthermore, students develop empathy because of relationship questions as they are able to see how the severity of their problem has affected their family and significant others. Subsequently, motivation may increase as they become cognizant of the impact their problem has had on other people in their lives.

## Scaling Questions

- On a scale of 1–10, with 1 being the lowest and 10 being the highest, where would you rate yourself in terms of reaching your goals that you identified last week?
- On a scale of 1–10, with 1 being that you never go to class and 10 being that you have perfect attendance, where would you put yourself? What would it take to increase two numbers on the scale?
- On a scale of 1–10, with 1 being that you are getting in trouble every day in class and 10 being that you are doing your school work and your teacher says something nice to you, where would you be?

The school social worker and other school professionals have the option to use scaling questions to quantify and measure the intensity of internal thoughts and feelings, along with helping the students to anchor reality and move forward from their problems (Franklin & Nurius, 1998; Pichot & Dolan, 2003). Many different variations of this technique can be used, such as asking for percentages of progress, holding up a ruler or string, or drawing a line on a sidewalk. Scaling questions are techniques used to determine where students are in terms of achieving their goals. Scaling is a subjective process, but it helps students to measure and to assess how much progress they may or may not have made toward goals. Typically, scaling questions have students rate where they are on a scale from 1 to 10 with 1 being the worst/lowest and 10 being the best/highest. Scaling is a technique that is familiar to most students and is a helpful tool for the therapist when students are having a difficult time seeing their progress.

Franklin, Corcoran, Nowicki, and Streeter (1997) describe three different uses of scaling in SFBT. First is to determine where the students are on the scale in terms of solving their own problems; second is to look for exceptions to the problem; and third is to construct a miracle or identify solution behaviors. The highest point on the scale should always represent the desired outcome. Furthermore, the scaling sequence must end with the social worker asking the students how they will move forward to another point on the scale.

## The Miracle Question

Now, I want to ask you a strange question. This is probably a question no one has asked you before. Suppose that while you are sleeping tonight, a miracle happens, and the problem that brought you here is solved. However, because you are sleeping, you don't know that the miracle has happened. So, when you wake up tomorrow morning, what will be the first thing that you notice that is different that will tell you a miracle has happened and that the problem which brought you here is solved?

The miracle question strengthens students' goals by allowing them to reconstruct their story, showing a future without the students' perceived problems (Berg & De Jong, 1996; De Jong & Berg, 2001). Moreover, the social worker uses the miracle question to help students identify ways in which the solution may already be occurring in their lives. According to Pichot and Dolan (2003), the miracle question came into being by chance. One of Berg's clients suggested, "Only a miracle will help," which enabled Berg and associates to realize the power of the client imagining how the future would be without the problem.

Pichot and Dolan (2003) describe five elements that are crucial to the miracle question. The first crucial element is saying the words "suppose a miracle happens." This tells the students that a desired change is possible. Second, the student must have a basic understanding of what the miracle is, which the statement "The problem that brought you here is solved" often defines. The third crucial element to the miracle question is immediacy. The miracle must be described as happening tonight and in an environment that is realistic for students, such as in their homes. Fourth, in the hypothetical situation, students must be unaware that the miracle has occurred. Without this, there is nothing for students to discover, which is a vital component of the miracle question. Fifth, students must recognize the signs that indicate to them that the miracle happened.

The miracle question provides students with a vision of a problem-free future and empowers them to learn new ways of behaving. Asking this question, very gently and thoughtfully, is believed to allow a shift in the students' usual thought processes (Pichot & Dolan, 2003).

## Goaling

*Goaling* is used as a verb in SFBT. An important distinction to make between goal setting in SFBT and other approaches to behavior change is that attaining the goal does not represent the end of counseling in SFBT; goals are considered the beginning of behavior change, not the end. The social worker and the student negotiate small, observable goals, set within a brief time frame, that lead to a new story for the student. The negotiation of goals should start immediately between the social worker and student (Franklin & Nurius, 1998). If a student is unable to think of a concrete goal, the practitioner may opt to provide multiple-choice answers. In addition, scaling questions are beneficial to measure the student's progress toward goal attainment. Three advantages of using scales in this context are that they make goals and actions that lead to goals, they place responsibility for change on students, and they allow students to take credit for the changes they make (Corcoran, 1998).

Walter and Peller (1996) say that goaling is the evolution of the meaning of what students want to experience or what their lives may be like after the alleviation of the problem. Goaling is talking about what students want to do; it is not problem solving, but creative and conversational (Walter & Peller, 1996). Furthermore, goaling allows the conversation to lead to areas in students' lives that are free of the problems and where students want their lives to be.

According to Sklare (1997), the two most common types of goals that students identify are positive and negative goals. *Positive goals* are stated in terms of what the student wants and are measurable. Typical examples are "I want to get better grades" or "I want to have more friends." Most positive goals lack specific behavioral details. Asking specific details about what students will be doing when they are moving toward that goal will help students identify specific behavioral details. So, the practitioner would say, "Let's just suppose your teacher was nicer to you. How would that help? What would you be doing differently?"

*Negative goals* are expressed as the absence of something. Students will usually want themselves to stop doing something or usually want someone else to stop doing something to them. Typical examples are "I want my parents to stop bothering me" or "I want to stop getting into fights at school." When faced with negative goals, social workers must help students reframe their goals in a way that gives students the responsibility. This can be accomplished by asking questions to help determine the students' motivation for wanting to stop doing something or wanting others to stop doing something to them. Some examples might be, "So when your parents aren't bothering you, what would that do for you?" or "When you're not getting into fights at school, what are you doing?"

## The Break for Reflection

The *break* is another integral part of SFBT. It helps transition the interview toward the final stage of the session, where the social worker or counselor develops a set of compliments for the student and a homework task. Most social workers will simply go to their desk and write down notes or just inform students that they need a minute to reflect on the discussion and make notes on their notepad. In schools, when interviews are informal and meeting places may be in classrooms or other areas, the social worker might go to the bathroom or just take some psychological space for a moment. What is important about the break is to create a strong psychological space so that when the social worker returns, the student is paying close attention to what the practitioner is going to say next (de Shazer, 1985). The social worker finishes the solution-focused session by giving the student a set of meaningful compliments, reviewing strengths and goals identified by the student, and developing a homework task to further encourage behavioral change.

## Case Example Illustrating Solution-Building Conversation

Box 4.1 provides an example of a solution-building conversation between a school-based practitioner and a 16-year-old student. A teacher has sent the student for help because he is sleeping during class, and she wants him to be taken out of her class because he will not participate.

The importance of this solution-building conversation is that the practitioner's dialogue with the student results in the student becoming more cooperative and selecting his own solution for the problem at hand. Notice also that the practitioner continually builds the relationship with the student, forming a desired goal to work on and asking the student to commit to the steps to accomplish the goal. This is an example of a solution-building process. The SFBT practitioner knows that this is only a small step but will seek to build on this cooperative beginning to help the student find ways to improve his behavior in the class. At the same time, the practitioner will work with the teacher to find out in detail what the teacher wants to see different in the student's behaviors. The practitioner might give an assignment to the teacher, like noticing when the student is doing what the teacher wants in the class.

## Soliciting Cooperation and Motivation in Students Who Resist

Staff in the school view most students at risk of dropping out as unmotivated, uncooperative, or resistant. SFBT practitioners believe that everyone has motivation and that people are in particular motivated toward personal goals. Every student has positive aspirations, and the solution-focused practitioner will tune into what those are with individual students. The focus is always on how the goal serves to motivate socially effective behaviors or positive interactions with others. SFBT views resistance as a normal human behavior. There are two types of resistance, active and passive. Every person has the ability to be resistant and uncooperative. At the same time, every person can be cooperative. Cooperation is something that can be facilitated when people have a relationship and are working together toward a win-win outcome. Facilitating cooperative behaviors increases the student's self-esteem and enables a true partnership between the practitioner and the student to emerge (Hawkes, Marsh, & Wilgosh, 1998).

**Box 4.1.** Case Example Illustrating
Solution-Building Conversation

*Student:* I hate that teacher. She makes a big deal out of everything. I was not sleeping. I was just resting my eyes for a second. What a liar she is. Nobody likes her.

*Social Worker:* So, you think the teacher does not understand what you were doing in her class.

S: Yeah, that's right. She is just trying to get rid of me.

SW: Trying to get rid of you?

S: Yeah, she does not like me at all.

SW: How is it that the teacher came not to like you?

S: I do not know. You'd have to ask her.

SW: What if I did ask her, what might she say?

S: I don't know. What kind of question is that?

SW: It is an imagination question. So, let's just imagine for a moment that you did know what she might say, what might it be?

S: That's dumb.

SW: You think so?

S: Yeah!

SW: Well, sometimes I might ask dumb questions, but it is okay to answer me anyway. So, what would the teacher say about not liking you? [waits in silence, does not give up on answer, smiles, remains pleasant with student]

S: Hmm. I guess she might say that I skip the beginning or end of her class. It is *boring*! But, this sleeping thing is stupid!

SW: Of course, I know the sleeping thing you do not agree with. You were just resting your eyes. Let me see if I have this right. She would say that she does not like you because you do not come on time and stay throughout the whole class?

S: Yeah, that is it.

SW: So, I guess she might also say she wants you to keep your eyes open in her class even if you want to rest them?

S: That is hard to do because she is a terrible teacher and I just can't listen. I think she should have to take her own class to see how terrible she is.

SW: Maybe that would help?

S: I do not know.

*SW:* So, tell me, which is more important to your teacher right now: keeping your eyes open or coming on time and staying to the end of her class?

*S:* I guess keeping my eyes open because she says she is going to put me in in-school suspension.

*SW:* How do you feel about going to in-school suspension? I have met students who prefer that to a class.

*S:* No! I am going to be in worse trouble if I have to go back there again. I might have to go to the alternative learning center, and my mom is going to be mad.

*SW:* So, you want to stay in the teacher's class?

*S:* Really, I want to be moved to another class but Mr. Jones [the principal] said that was not going to happen.

*SW:* So, your choices are to stay in the teacher's class by finding a way to keep your eyes open or to go to the alternative learning center and face your mom?

*S:* It sucks!

*SW:* Yeah, it is a tough situation. I can see how you would feel frustrated. So, have there been times that you have somehow managed to keep your eyes open in the teacher's class?

*S:* Yeah.

*SW:* Tell me about those times.

*S:* Well, sometimes when it was interesting or she was reviewing for a test.

*SW:* You mean, sometimes the class is actually interesting? When would those times be?

*S:* Like when she is not lecturing and we are working on a group project.

*SW:* So, those times your eyes are wide open and you are participating too?

*S:* Yeah, I guess so.

*SW:* You said before that you did not close your eyes for too long. I bet sometimes in the past you managed to keep your eyes open even when she was lecturing and super-boring.

*S:* Yeah, I did.

*SW:* So, what percent of the time are you able to keep your eyes open? 5%? 10%? 25%?

*(continued)*

47

## Box 4.1. (*Continued*)

S:   80% of the time!

SW:  Wow! Even when she is boring.

S:   Yeah, I think so.

SW:  So, tell me, what percent do you think your teacher would give you?.

S:   Not as high because she blows everything up.

SW:  Yes, of course. Well, just suppose she improved a little and gave you more of a fair rating. What might she say?

S:   Maybe about 50 or 60%.

SW:  That is pretty good. How do you think you can get to 90%?

S:   Get more sleep so I can stand her boring lectures.

SW:  Let's just suppose you did get some more sleep. How might that help?

S:   I think it would just make me more alert and patient.

SW:  Are there any other things that keep you from being alert and patient? Like, for example, a lot of students I know smoke a joint or take medications before class and that makes them sleepy. Or they might have fights with their parents or girlfriend that make them distracted.

S:   No, I don't smoke before class. My mom makes me take my ADHD medicine but that does not make me sleepy.

SW:  For my information, how much sleep do you usually get per night?

S:   About 3–4 hours.

SW:  What do you do instead of sleeping?

S:   Listen to the stereo and watch TV. Sometimes talk to my friends in the chat room if I can sneak into my mom's computer room.

SW:  So, how much extra sleep do you think you would need to keep your eyes open in this class?

S:   I do not know. Maybe 2–3 hours more.

SW:  So, maybe 5–6 hours?

S:   Yeah.

SW:  What about the teacher's percentage? What would she say you could do to get to 60 or 70%?

S:   I think she likes it when I stay in the class and ask questions.

SW: You have done that before?

S: Yeah, sometimes.

SW: If you did that, would that get you to 70% with the teacher?

S: Maybe.

[At this point, the social worker tells the student that she is going to take a few moments to think about what has been said and write down some notes]

SW: Well, you know, I am really impressed that you are able to keep your eyes open in a class that you feel is boring and that you find ways to stay in the class and ask questions in the class. How do you manage to do that?

S: I just do it. I am not always a bad student.

SW: No, I am hearing that you know how to be a good student and that you do not want to go to the alternative learning center. I wonder if you can try an experiment for just this week? Get 5–6 hours of sleep so you can have the patience and alertness to keep your eyes open all the time during the class. Also, do what you suggested. Stay in the class from the beginning to the end. Ask questions during class. See if that will keep the teacher from kicking you out of her class.

S: Okay, I could try that.

SW: So, you could try that?

S: Yeah.

SW: So, just so I am clear about your plan for staying in the class, tell me again what you plan to do. I want to write it down here in my notes. I will talk to you at the end of the week to see how it is working.

[Student rehearses plan and social worker asks about details of the suggested approach]

SFBT practitioners take a curious position, or "not knowing approach," when working with students who are actively resisting. They find ways to agree with the students' points of view and do not actively confront the students on points of greatest resistance. This serves to disarm students. For example, if you are playing tug-of-war with someone and stop tugging back, they often lose their balance and stop pulling against you. SFBT practitioners use the same principle in managing passive resistance. When a student gives passive responses to questions, such as "I don't know," it is important for the practitioner to pretend that she is too slow to understand and must rephrase the question. These types of conversational tactics are meant to keep the conversation and relationship moving forward in the face of resistance.

## Using Emotions to Engage and Motivate Students

Sometimes SFBT practitioners will construct positive engagement by prefacing their questions about what students are doing or might do to change, coupled with acknowledging their expressions of emotions and using those emotions as a catalyst for change (Miller & de Shazer, 2000). The emotional states that SFBT practitioners are most likely to use are those associated with positive aspirations, goals, wants, and desires. They will also juxtapose positive feelings and desires against feelings and outcomes that the student wishes to avoid. This is illustrated in the solution-focused conversation in Box 4.1. In the example, the student wanted to remain in the class to avoid the consequences of going to the alternative learning center and facing the anger of his mom. The fears about the consequences of his behavior were used as a way to focus the student on a more positive outcome.

In another example, a student may say that she hates the school and does not like to attend but at the same time say that she really wants to graduate so she can get a better job. The SFBT practitioner would focus on the positive feeling and desire to graduate and ask questions about how that became an important goal in her life. The counselor would be curious about how the student came to feel a desire to graduate, for example. How strong is that feeling? Who else in her social network or family shares that feeling? Are there any people who do not share that feeling about the importance of graduation? How does the student keep the positive desire when others are negative? The practitioner might also assess the strength and importance of the desire to graduate through a scaling question: "On a scale of 0–10, with 0 meaning you do not care that much whether you graduate or not and 10 being that you care a great deal and are ready to do about anything to make that happen, where would you say you are?" In addition, practitioners might make statements like "Some students do not feel like they want to graduate or just give up. What makes you feel differently?" Such statements are aimed at complimenting and encouraging the student and increasing her positive feelings and desires toward graduation.

# Tools and Practice Examples

Franklin et al. (2001) suggest that, in order to conduct SFBT, the school social workers and other mental health practitioners must follow a solution-focused process and, at a minimum, implement the miracle question, ask scaling questions, and provide compliments. An SFBT session format is flexible enough to adapt to the individual needs of each student but also structured enough to provide guidance to practitioners. In this section, we describe the structure of an SFBT counseling session and illustrate several of the counseling techniques.

A typical session follows the structure discussed by Franklin and Moore (1999):

Warm-up conversation to establish rapport and create relaxed environment

Identifying problem and tracking new exceptions to the problem

Using relationship questions to examine student's perception of how others view student's problem or problem resolution

Asking scaling questions and coping questions

Building goals and discovering solutions by asking the miracle question

Taking a break to formulate compliments and homework

Giving compliments and homework tasks

## Structure of the Interview and Case Example

Most solution-focused interviews occur during traditional 50-minute sessions. In schools, however, these interviews may last for shorter periods of time. Interviews may last 20–30 minutes, for example. The structure of the interview is divided into three parts. The first part is usually spent making small talk with the student to find out a little bit about the student's life. During this first part, the social worker should be looking to understand the student's interests, motivations, competencies, and belief systems.

*Social Worker:* Hello, Charles. I understand your teacher, Mrs. Park, sent you here to see me because you're at risk of failing out of school. But I'd like to hear from you the reason you are here to see me and how this can help you. [allows student to state what the problem is]

*Student:* I don't know. I hate this school, and I just want to drop out so that people will leave me alone.

*SW:* So, if I'm understanding you correctly, you're here to see me because you hate the school and a lot of people—your teachers and maybe your parents—have been bugging you about your grades and doing homework?

*S:* Yeah.

*SW:* So what sorts of things do you like to do when you're not in school?

*S:* Ummm, I like to hang out with my friends.

*SW:* What do you and your friends talk about when you're hanging out?

*S:* I don't know. We talk about basketball and music and stuff. [social worker will continue to develop rapport and try to find out student's interests and belief systems]

The second part of the session, which takes up the bulk of the time—around 40 minutes in traditional sessions but maybe less time in-school interviews—is spent discussing the problem, looking for exceptions, and formulating goals. One of the key components to SFBT that has been emphasized in this chapter is working with the student to identify the problem, to look for times when the problem is absent, to look for ways the solution is already occurring, and to develop attainable goals to help resolve the problem. The second part is usually initiated with questions like "How can I help you?" or "What is the reason you have come to see me?" or "How will you know when counseling is no longer necessary?" (Sklare, 1997).

SW: Okay, so how can I help you, or what can you get out of our meeting today so that you know it's been worth your time to see me?

S: I want my teachers and my parents to stop bugging me about my grades and doing homework. This school is just a waste of my time and my classes are stupid.

SW: Have you had a class that you didn't think was stupid or a waste of time? [example of looking for exceptions]

S: My English class last year was cool because we got to read some interesting books and have good discussions about them.

SW: What made the books interesting and the discussions good?

S: Well, they were books that I could understand and relate to. My teacher also made the time and effort to explain things to us and made sure we all got a turn to speak our thoughts.

SW: You said you hated this school, but yet you haven't dropped out yet. How have you managed to do that? [allows student to identify possible solutions and possible successes in what they've already been doing]

S: Well, I'm still going to some of my classes, but at this point I just don't care any more.

SW: Charles, for those classes that you do attend, what would your teachers say about your academic work? [example of relationship question]

S: I guess they might say that I don't pay attention in class, that I don't do my homework, and that I'm not trying.

SW: Do you agree with that?

S: I guess, but it's just that the classes are so stupid and boring.

SW: Charles, I'd like to ask you an unusual question. It's probably something no one has ever asked you before. Suppose, after we're done and you leave my office, you go to bed tonight and a miracle happens. This miracle solves all of your problems that brought you here today, but because you were sleeping, you didn't know it occurred. So, the next morning you wake up and you sense something is different. What will you notice that is different that lets you know this miracle occurred and your problems are solved? [example of the miracle question]

S: I guess I wouldn't be cutting class and maybe getting better grades.

SW: What will you be doing differently to get better grades?

S: I would probably be better prepared for class.

SW: What does being better prepared for class look like? [continue to probe and elicit more details and examples]

S: I'd pay attention in class and take some notes.

SW: What else would you be doing differently when you're getting better grades?

S: Probably doing my homework and not causing trouble in class with the teacher.

SW: So, what will you be doing instead of causing trouble in class?

S: Listen and sit there and take notes, I guess.

SW: So, on a scale from 1 to 10, with 1 being I'm dropping out of school no matter what and 10 being the miracle solved my problems and I'm going to graduate, where would you say you are right now? [example of a scaling question]

S: Three.

SW: What sorts of things prevent you from giving it a 2 or a 1?

S: Well, I know I need to get my high school diploma because I always thought I might go study how to be a med tech at college. I like the TV show "CSI" and want to work in forensics.

SW: Wow! You want to study forensics. So, you need to finish school for that. So, what would need to happen for you to be a 4 or a 5?

S: I'd need to start coming to classes and doing my work. [examples of student identifying goals and solutions. Social worker would continue looking for solutions that are already occurring in Charles's life and collaborate on identifying and setting small, attainable goals]

The final part of the session lasts around 5–10 minutes. This last part involves giving the student a set of compliments, homework, and determining whether to continue discussing this topic at another time. In school settings, practitioners such as teachers and social workers have separated this last part from the rest of the conversation. The break, for example, might be extended, and the conversation might pick up in a different class period or at a different time of the day (e.g., before and after lunch).

SW: I'd like to take a minute to write down some notes based on what we've talked about. Is there anything else you feel I should know before I take this quick break?

S: No.

SW: [after taking a break] Well, Charles, I'd like to compliment you on your commitment to staying in school despite your frustrations. You seem like a bright student and understand the importance of finishing high

S:    school. I'd like to meet with you again to continue our work together. Would that be all right with you?

S:    Sure.

SW:   So, for next week, I'd like you to try and notice when things are going a little bit better in your classes and what you're doing differently during those times.

### Internet Resources for Solution-Focused Schools

Brief Family Therapy Center: www.brief-therapy.org

Cynthia Franklin: www.utexas.edu/ssw/faculty/ franklin

Garza High School: A Solution-Focused High School: http://www. austinschools.org/garza

## Key Points to Remember

Youths from all backgrounds and in every place are at risk of dropping out of school. This challenge is compounded further by a lack of evidence-based interventions that school social workers and other practitioners can use to reach this challenging population.

SFBT is one intervention that can help school social workers and other school professionals engage and retrieve dropout youths. This approach builds on student strengths. SFBT offers conversational, questioning techniques that help practitioners to engage students in a solution-building process. A solution-building process helps students discover goals, tasks, and behaviors that can change future outcomes.

The SFBT practitioner acts as a catalyst or facilitator and creates an interpersonal context where solutions emerge from students and their ideas.

SFBT also provides specific skills for engaging, motivating, and eliciting cooperation in resistant students. Techniques include going with resistance; focusing on personal goals, taking a curious, not-knowing approach; playing dumb; and reinforcing positive emotions.

The structure of the SFBT counseling session has three parts. Case examples have given an overview of the parts and how SFBT can be used to help students at risk of dropping out.

# Working With First Nations Students and Families

*Dorie J. Gilbert*
*Gail H. Sims*

## Getting Started

The number of U.S. persons estimated to be partly or fully of American Indian or Alaska Native heritage is approximately 4.1 million, or 1.5% of the U.S. population (Ogunwole, 2002). This group is one of the fastest growing populations because of increased birth rates, decreased infant mortality rates, and a greater willingness to report Native ancestry. Although the terms "American Indian," "Indian," and "Native American" are commonly used, they represent European-imposed, colonized names that serve to oppress indigenous, First Nations, or Native people, the original people occupying lands now called the United States (Yellow Bird, 2001). In this chapter, except when quoting or describing programs, we use the terms "First Nations" or "Native people" interchangeably to refer to the group as a whole; however, when addressing individuals, the best practice is to refer to Native people by their tribal nation or indigenous affiliation.

First Nations people represent a diverse population across the United States. Most (66%) Native people reside in metropolitan areas rather than on reservations or defined tribal areas, and nationally, there are 550 federally recognized tribes with a multitude of distinct tribal languages (Yellow Bird, 2001). As a group, they have experienced collective disenfranchisement, historical trauma, and contemporary challenges to traditional ways of life (Brave Heart, 1998, 2001a, 2001b). School social workers should be knowledgeable about how risks to the psychosocial well-being of Native people are rooted in impoverished living conditions and traumatic life events associated with oppression and loss of traditional culture and identity.

Within this complex array of distressed living, a number of mental health, social, and behavioral problems as well as protective factors have been identified among Native children. In comparison to the majority culture, Native children may be at greater risk for a variety of emotional and behavioral disorders and negative psychosocial conditions. Native children enter kindergarten or first grade with relatively low levels of oral language, prereading, and premathematics skills, and less general knowledge (Farkas, 2003). Teachers in both tribal and public schools identified the three most serious problems for Native children as parental alcohol and drug abuse, poverty, and lack of parental involvement (Pavel, 1995). Other problems often cited as affecting Native children include suicidal behavior, substance abuse, violence, and depression; however, these problems must be considered within the context of complicated economic and social-political conditions, namely, the larger issues of past and current oppression, extreme poverty, loss of cultural identity, and historical trauma (Brave Heart, 2001a; Weaver, 2001).

Strengths and protective factors among Native children and adolescents include factors retained from the original culture. These include strong family bonds; emphasis on well-being of the community; wisdom and guidance of elders; cultural practices and traditions that serve to heal, empower, and increase positive ethnic identity; and sovereignty, the formalized self-determination of reservations to make choices (Weaver, 2001).

Many school social workers are in need of guidance in working with Native people; few service providers are specifically trained to work with this population. This chapter should assist school social workers and school-oriented mental health professionals in understanding how best to address the psychosocial needs of indigenous children within the school setting.

# What We Know

The literature on effective interventions with First Nations people is growing but is far from an established evidence-based guide to practice with Native people, especially with regard to school-based services. Moreover, Yellow Horse and Brave Heart (2004) note that there is a "dichotomy between evidence-based models alleged to be effective with American Indian/Alaska Native populations, and culturally grounded American Indian/Alaska Natives models whose efficacy have not been demonstrated" (p. 35). Rather, nationally recognized evidence-based programs are often not used with Native populations or are used with little or no integration of cultural congruency. On the other hand, culturally based programs designed and implemented by and for Native people often show great promise but lack the replications needed to become nationally recognized as evidence based.

The best practices at this time are "promising practices" that draw on conventional or some combination of conventional and cultural practices but are sufficiently flexible to incorporate the cultural norms and values of Native people.

# What We Can Do

### Counseling and Therapeutic Interventions
*Cognitive Behavioral Therapy (CBT) for Child Traumatic Stress* (Schinke, Brounstein, & Garner, 2001) addresses trauma-related psychiatric symptoms in children aged 3–18 years. Randomized control trials showed significantly greater reductions in post-traumatic stress disorder (PTSD), depression, anxiety, problem behaviors,

and parental emotional distress. Given its focus on traumatic stress and reported high incidence of trauma among Native adolescents, it may have utility for Native populations (Yellow Horse & Brave Heart, 2004).

*Family systems therapy* matches well with the Native worldview of family and community collectivism. It sees family as the most important social unit, and at the same time, requires family members to explore ways in which their own behavior may be maladaptive or injurious to other family members (LaFromboise & Dizon, 2003).

*Social cognitive therapy* incorporates new developments, including the recognition of the impact of culture on personal agency (Bandura, 2002) and incorporation of family systems therapy and constructivist theory (Franklin & Jordan, 2003). In particular, constructivism—which emphasizes the personal realities, individual worldviews, and personal meanings of the client—strengthens the potential success of social cognitive therapy with Native people.

## School-Based Programs

Most school-based programs are group-level prevention models and are recommended for use in conjunction with individual and/or family-based interventions. These programs primarily target areas such as drug or alcohol abuse, HIV, youth violence, suicide prevention, cultural identity building, and parent–child functioning (Sanchez-Way & Johnson, 2000).

*PATHS (Promoting Alternative Thinking Strategies)* is an evidence-based classroom program using cognitive skill building to assist schoolchildren with identifying and regulating their emotions toward increasing social functioning and reducing acting out and aggression.

*Family and Schools Together* (FAST) promotes protective factors to improve family functioning for children aged 4–12 years with behavioral and academic problems.

*Native Liaison Programs* represent a highly promising strategy for working with Native children in school districts. A Native liaison is a person who works directly with the school district and acts a liaison between Native families and the school system. This position can be funded by the Office of Indian Education through a formula grant available to any school district with at least 10 Indian children who are members of a state-recognized or federally recognized tribe or who have a parent or grandparent who is a member of a state-recognized or federally recognized tribe. Though the overall purpose of these grants is to assist Native children in meeting state academic standards, most programs recognize the interrelatedness of students' mental health needs and academic performance.

## Culturally Grounded Interventions

Culturally appropriate interventions are grounded in indigenous culture and may include activities such as learning traditional languages and crafts, activities that increase positive cultural identity and/or spiritual practices such as talking circles, dream work, and purification lodges (Sanchez-Way & Johnson, 2000). Yellow Horse and Brave Heart (2004) identified the following culturally congruent programs that are promising practices for Native youths:

*Storytelling for Empowerment* is a program designed for middle school rural or reservation Native children and Latino youth. The program aims to increase resiliency by decreasing substance abuse and other risk factors such as confused cultural identity and lack of positive parental role model.

*Zuni Life Skills Curriculum,* used with Zuni Pueblo adolescents, merges social cognitive, life-skills development with peer helping to increase social-emotional competence and decrease suicidal risks. Evaluation results indicate reduced suicide probability and significant reductions in hopelessness.

*Historical Trauma and Unresolved Grief Intervention* (HTUG) is a psychoeducational group intervention that targets parents, with the overall goal of reducing mental health risk factors and increasing protective factors for Native children (Brave Heart, 1998, 2001a, 2001b).

References, contact information, and suggested readings related to the aforementioned programs are included in the References section.

## Steps in Implementing the Best Intervention(s)

This section includes a summary (in steps) of how to implement a promising intervention, social cognitive therapy, available for addressing the problems of Native children in the school system. Though no one intervention can be recommended at the time, we have chosen to feature social cognitive therapy because of its flexibility and ability to incorporate cultural constructs important to Native people, including

- flexibility to include others, such as family members and community liaisons, in the helping process;
- flexibility to include culturally based helping processes, specifically indigenous healing processes where they may apply to the child/adolescent/ family;
- a focus on trauma and stress, issues relevant to Native families;
- a recognition of the racial or ethnic, cultural, and socioeconomic diversity of Native families; and
- an emphasis on social construction, that is, on the personal realities, individual worldviews, and personal meanings of the child or family.

Social cognitive therapy, as presented here, involves seven major steps:

- Step 1: *Establish contact with a Native liaison.* Utilize the natural skills of a Native liaison. If your school district does not have a Native liaison, inquire about how to establish such a position at the district level.
- Step 2: *Self and Client Assessment*

*Self-assess.* Be clear that you understand general differences between Native belief systems and dominant culture belief systems. Engage in self-assessment to be grounded in your own personal and professional values and commitment to culturally competent practice. Note how larger societal oppression affects the lives of children, families, and larger Native communities. This includes understanding the effects of historical trauma and unresolved grief (Brave Heart, 1998, 2001a, 2001b) on Native families.

Assess *cultural orientation of client.* Assess the child's or family's comfort level with mainstream interventions. The comfort level of Native people with mainstream counseling practices ranges from acceptance to total rejection in favor of traditional native healing practices, with many falling in the middle of this range. Native people come from diverse backgrounds and cultural orientations; most are bicultural, meaning they are able to operate from both mainstream and Native cultural orientations.

Assess *validity of previous or current diagnoses.* Eurocentric assessments can be detrimental and inappropriate for Native populations and usually stem from a practitioner's bias and/or lack of awareness of cultural differences and/or culturally biased measurement and assessment instruments (Gilbert, 2003). Ideally, assessments of Native people should use culture-specific tests, measures of cultural/ethnic identity and acculturative stress/trauma as moderators of standardized tests, thematic apperception types of tests, and, when possible, qualitative and multiple assessment strategies (Gilbert, 2003).

- Step 3: *Research the specific cultural practices and traditions of the tribe or community.* Not all families are affiliated with a tribe or Native community. However, most have some connection to a larger community, whether through other families or participation in tribal events associated with one or more Native communities. Find out the specific cultural practices and traditions of the tribe or community to which the child or family is most connected. Make note of the resources, coping abilities, and personal meanings the child or family and community bring to the situation. Be aware that with many Native communities, counseling is best accomplished within a family context. Native children tend to acquiesce to elders (including school counselors and personnel), and little will be accomplished without involving the family so that the child has permission from elders to express himself or herself.

- Step 4: *Establish credibility and trustworthiness.* Credibility begins with accomplishing the aforementioned steps. Building trust involves patience and flexibility. In the initial session, begin by engaging in nonthreatening material. Be unobtrusive, make silent observations, show humility, and allow for differences, especially with regard to time. In a traditional

Native view, time is flowing and relative, which from a Eurocentric perspective may be viewed as being irresponsible with respect to time. Schedule longer sessions to account for family involvement and allow ample time for narrative expressions, keeping in mind the fluidity of time in traditional Native culture and a tendency for Native clients to "drop by" (Brave Heart, 2001b). You may also consider incorporating humor with Native people, or at least be aware that they may introduce their problem with a joke or a story. A generic suggestion is to incorporate Native themes and values (e.g., love of nature, legends, colors, animals) as a way to broach topics. In addition, the liaison can assist with building the rapport with families. Beginning with a brief, relevant self-disclosure is also helpful as a way to open communication and show relatedness. The idea is to establish a relationship and to provide a model for sharing information, especially when dealing with children.

- Step 5: *Solicit information and develop a definition of the problem from the child's or family's cultural point of view.* Avoid asking for written information. Techniques for soliciting information through narratives, storytelling, and indirect communication styles are relevant for Native communication styles. Mirroring is extremely important. For one, it provides the practitioner a way of altering his or her interactions based on how the child or family interacts. For example, individual differences in Native communication styles, such as indirect or direct eye contact, should be mirrored rather than basing one's interactions on assumptions or stereotypes.

- Step 6: *Explore client's thoughts, including client's cues and reinforcements for negative behavior.* Keep in mind that the child or family may not view behavior as maladaptive. Establish an understanding of the constructs, meaning, and value associated with the behavior.

- Step 7: *Effect change in maladaptive behavior*
  *Provide information, models, and opportunities for the child or family to master the necessary skills.* Storytelling and imaginary play are recommended for use with the Native children and adolescents. It is useful to share experiences of others who have overcome similar situations. In keeping with an indirect communication style, models of behavior should be presented as suggestions.
  *Explore successes and failures with behavior change.* Praise any successes with behavior change. Address previously failed attempts and explore individual and environmental factors that have contributed to unsuccessful attempts.
  *Incorporate a group experience.* If possible, arrange for the child or family to meet with similar others who have experience with the behavior

and endorse its effectiveness. A culturally congruent group program offers an opportunity to increase positive cultural identity and indigenous healing while promoting prosocial activities, shared responsibility, networks, and collective approaches.

# Tools and Practice Examples

Eddie Snow Wolf is a 14-year-old Native 9th-grade student at Smith High School, a predominantly white and low-to-middle-income public high school in the Southwest. Eddie has been at the school for 5 months, and he is struggling with the course work and having difficulty getting along with classmates. Eddie came to the attention of the school social worker, Ms. Esther Jones, after he was expelled for fighting. The vice principal referred Eddie to Ms. Jones because he felt that "some home problems" might be causing Eddie's academic and conduct problems.

## Step 1: Establish Contact With a Native Liaison
Ms. Jones contacted Michael Stone, the school district's Native liaison. Ms. Jones met with Mr. Stone to brief him on what details were known about Eddie's situation, and in turn Mr. Stone briefed her on what he knew of the tribe, the Oglala Lakota, to which Eddie belonged.

## Step 2: Self and Client Assessment
### Self-Assessment
Ms. Jones, a 35-year-old Euro-American female, acknowledged that she had no experience working with Native populations but had read resource material with general information about Native cultural norms versus mainstream, Eurocentric norms. In addition, she understood how oppression and poverty influenced the lives of many Native families.

### Assess Cultural Orientation of Client
Ms. Jones reviewed Eddie's school and transfer records and determined that just prior to entering Smith High, he had lived on a nearby reservation, and from the records, he had attended a public, nontribal school only in 6th and 7th grades. From this, she made a tentative judgment that, on a continuum, Eddie might be more aligned with traditional Native practices and somewhat uncomfortable with Eurocentric, mainstream interventions.

### Assess Validity of Current and Previous Diagnoses
Ms. Jones noted that 2 years prior, when Eddie attended public school, he was identified as likely having attention deficit disorder (ADD). Knowing that Native children are often misdiagnosed, Ms. Jones decided to reevaluate the diagnosis with Mr. Stone's help.

## Step 3: Research the Specific Cultural Practices and Traditions of the Tribe or Community

Mr. Stone helped Ms. Jones to research the Oglala Lakota People. Ms. Jones learned that in that tradition, communication with families is usually done along gender lines, and respect must be given to cross-gender interactions (Brave Heart, 2001b). Should both a male and female family member of Eddie's family attend the counseling session, she, as a woman, would first address the other female before addressing the male. The tribal community is very strong, with most people living in the nearby urban community but visiting the reservation frequently for cultural events. With the tribal communities, families and extended families are closely connected. A particular tribal practice is for the eldest male relative to take on the title and role of "grandfather" or "father" to younger family members. Another Lakota way of life involves a concept of *tiospaye* (a collection of related families) in which a group of blood and nonblood relatives meet as a group to discuss how to strengthen the family. Ms. Jones and Mr. Stone also recognized that Eddie's immediate family members would need to be contacted to attend the counseling, based on their understanding that many traditional Native children will not disclose personal information without the presence or permission of parents or elders.

## Step 4: Establishing Credibility and Trustworthiness

At the first meeting, Ms. Jones and Mr. Stone met with Eddie and Eddie's grandfather, the only immediate family member available for the meeting. Eddie's older sister lived in a nearby city and wanted to attend but did not have transportation. The meeting was scheduled for 90 minutes rather than the usual 1 hour. On the basis of Lakota practices, Ms. Jones first allowed Mr. Stone to address the grandfather. After that introduction, Ms. Jones began with a brief, informal self-disclosure. She talked about her own grandfather and how important it was for him to be involved in her life. Ms. Jones and Mr. Stone then invited Mr. Snow Wolf to discuss his role in Eddie's life. Through this they learned that Mr. Snow Wolf is Eddie's deceased father's uncle, the eldest living male. As she listened and learned about the family history, Ms. Jones discovered that Eddie's mother and father had died in a car accident 2 years earlier. She was able to connect this information to Eddie's school records and recognized that the loss of his parents coincided with teachers' identifying him as needing to be tested for ADD.

## Step 5: Solicit Information

Slowly, Ms. Jones broached the topic of the fight, the reason that Eddie was expelled from school. Using indirect communication, she first talked about how school environments can be difficult at times for teens. She asked Eddie how he experienced the school as being difficult. Eddie disclosed that he felt the teachers at the school did not care about the Native students and that they ignored other students when they called Natives names. Through this conversation, it was revealed that Eddie's fight started after he had been repeatedly harassed by a white male classmate who called Eddie a "squaw boy." Eddie felt that although the teacher heard the classmate use this term repeatedly, the teacher failed to reprimand him. Eddie felt he had to take matters into his own hands to defend himself and his honor.

### Step 6: Exploring Clients' Thoughts, Including Clients' Cues and Reinforcements for Negative Behavior

Ms. Jones explored what Eddie meant by "defend himself" and learned that the term "squaw boy" is a derogatory term and that by using it, the classmate was insulting Eddie and his entire family. It insulted his manhood and was especially hurtful because he came from a strong lineage of warriors. Ms. Jones learned that in Eddie's view, anyone should know that this is a derogatory slur and that the teacher should have recognized this and reprimanded the other student.

### Step 7: Effecting Change in Maladaptive Behavior

#### Provide Information and Opportunities for the Student and Family to Master the Necessary Skills

Ms. Jones continued to meet with Eddie over the next week to discuss strategies he could use in handling conflicts with students. She asked Eddie to practice these skills and scheduled a second meeting with Eddie and his grandfather.

The next week, Ms. Jones received a phone call from Eddie's older sister. She wanted to know what was going on with Eddie. In the conversation, the sister said that Eddie and his grandfather were living in a trailer and often went without food. She wanted to know what resources were available for them but warned that they would not want anyone, not even the counselor, to know about their financial struggles. That same day, Eddie's grandfather dropped in to see Ms. Jones. Understanding that this type of "drop in" might occur, Ms. Jones made the time to see him and offered him coffee. The grandfather wanted to talk about Eddie's drinking problem. Ms. Jones thanked him for stopping in and listened carefully as he described how Eddie drinks in the evenings and doesn't complete his schoolwork. He wanted to know what programs were available. Ms. Jones said that she would research this. She also took the opportunity to tell him that his granddaughter, Eddie's sister, was worried that he was not eating and not staying strong enough to take care of Eddie. Mr. Snow Wolf did not respond, but when Ms. Jones handed him a piece of paper with a list of places he could go for food and other resources, he nodded and thanked her. Ms. Jones set up an appointment with the family and Mr. Stone for the following week.

### Explore Successes and Failures With Behavior Change

In that session, Ms. Jones explored how Eddie was handling the dynamics of the classroom. She explored his successes and discussed more strategies. To move into the topic of substance abuse, she and Mr. Stone followed steps 5 and 6. Mr. Stone broached the topic of substance abuse by telling stories of similar students who had overcome substance abuse problems.

### Incorporate a Group Experience

Ms. Jones researched and found a group-based substance abuse program for Lakota youth. Since Eddie was an enrolled member of the tribe, the program was free. Also, the program incorporated Native healing practices and included a cultural identity component that would support Eddie's sense of positive ethnic identity.

## Key Points to Remember

School social workers should be knowledgeable about how risks to the psychosocial well-being of Native children, adolescents, and families are often rooted in collective disenfranchisement, historical trauma, and contemporary challenges associated with loss of traditional culture and identity.

Strong family and community bonds, wisdom and guidance of elders, and positive cultural practices, traditions, and ethnic identity are among the recognized strengths and protective factors for Native children and adolescents.

In the absence of an established evidence-based guide to practice with Native people in school settings, we recommend "promising practices" that draw on conventional or some combination of conventional and cultural practices and are sufficiently flexible to incorporate the cultural norms and values of Native people. Promising practices include a number of counseling and therapeutic techniques, school-based programs, and culturally grounded interventions.

This chapter highlights social cognitive therapy because of its flexibility and ability to incorporate cultural constructs important to Native children and families. A seven-step process of social cognitive therapy provides details on culturally relevant client assessment, information gathering, establishment of credibility and trustworthiness, exploration of problems and thoughts, and ultimately, methods of effecting the desired change in behavior. A case study further elucidates how these seven steps are accomplished.

The authors would like to thank Dawn Echo Romero, CACIII, LCDC, for her review and assistance with the chapter. Romero (who is part Oglala-Sincangu Lakota) has provided substance abuse counseling for youth and their families for 14 years in both Colorado and Texas.

# Home Visiting

## 6

Essential Guidelines for Home Visits
and Engaging With Families

*Barbara Hanna Wasik*
*Gary L. Shaffer*

*Visiting with people in their homes is one of the most humane and
family-centered approaches to service delivery in our society. Home visiting is
uniquely supportive of family life, bringing services to families, providing services
in a familiar setting, and reducing obstacles to services.*

*Wasik & Bryant, 2001*

## Getting Started

Home visiting has a long history in education, family and child welfare, and physical
and mental health services (Hancock & Pelton, 1989; Levine & Levine, 1970;
Oppenheimer, 1925; Richmond, 1899). Home visits are critical in serving children and youth from birth to high school and in addressing issues ranging from
programs for preschool children through school system concerns. Educational
organizations rely on home visits to address a wide range of issues related to
student behaviors such as attendance, discipline, physical or mental challenges,
drug or alcohol abuse, depression, or antisocial activities. Other home visits
focus on student characteristics relating specifically to school performance, such
as risk for school failure among preschool children or low academic achievement
among school-aged children.

Why this enduring interest in and reliance on home visiting? Many believe that
home visits help break down barriers between professionals and families, reduce
obstacles to services, and provide opportunities to respond to individual family
needs. Minuchin, Colapinto, and Minuchin (1998) have written that, through
home visiting, "the aura of authority that characterizes an official setting is muted
and the reality of the family's life environment is acknowledged" (p. 204). By visiting homes, home visitors can gain an appreciation of the family's home life and
can respond with more knowledge and greater sensitivity to the family's needs.
Through their presence in the family's community, they can gain knowledge about
the local culture, values, and languages. They also gain unique opportunities for
engaging families. Regardless of the impetus for the home visit, home visitors

need not only general knowledge and skills related to home visiting (including a repertoire of appropriate clinical/interviewing skills) but also specific knowledge and skills related to the particular focus of the visit.

Today, home visiting remains a mainstay of varied services, including early childhood intervention; nursing, rehabilitation, and hospice programs; protective services; and school social work practice. Young children and their parents are served through an extensive set of national programs, such as the Parents as Teachers, Healthy Families America, Nurse–Family Partnership, Home Instruction for Parents of Preschool Youngsters, and Early Head Start programs. In addition, hundreds of local parent support programs have included home-visiting strategies (Catalano, Berglund, Ryan, Lonczak, & Hawkins, 2002; Fraser, Day, Galinsky, Hodges, & Smokowski, 2004; Gomby, Culross, & Behrman 1999; Greenberg, Domitrovich, & Bumbarger, 2001). Some of these programs have been intensely researched and tested; others have been implemented with little research or empirical evidence to guide their efforts. Some programs employ professionals as home visitors while others employ paraprofessionals. Other critical differences among these programs include the goals of the home visit, the procedures and materials used, the duration and intensity of the visits, and whether participation is voluntary.

In this chapter, we present information relevant for school social workers and others who provide services to school-aged students and their families. We begin with providing information on the prevalence of home visiting and a brief review of program outcomes. We then include guidelines for home visiting, specific information for preparing for a home visit, and a framework and strategies to guide the actual home visit. Additional resources are included to illustrate the various types of programs, purposes, and outcomes of home visitation.

# What We Know

## Prevalence of Home Visiting

The acceptance of home visiting as an effective practice among school social workers is illustrated in a random sample of school social workers who were asked about school violence and personal safety. A vast majority of the 576 respondents (91%) endorsed home visits as an effective intervention for aggressive children, and 82% of those who responded reported that they conduct home visits for aggressive children. This high rate of home visiting occurred despite the fact that 74% of respondents viewed home visits as potentially dangerous situations (Astor, Behre, Wallace, & Fravil, 1998).

Further evidence of the widespread use of home visiting across agencies comes from Johnson's study (2001). She found 37 states reporting the use of home-visiting programs to improve parenting skills (81%), enhance child development

(76%), and prevent abuse and neglect (71%). Several states (i.e., Florida, Illinois, Michigan, New York, Ohio, Oklahoma, and Washington) have demonstrated their commitment to home visiting by budgeting $10–50 million a year for one or more such programs. Johnson (2001) concluded:

> The convergence of several policy and research trends created a policy setting conducive to the expansion of home visiting efforts. These include growing public awareness of infant and brain development research, emphasis on early education and school readiness, recognition of the importance of family support, enactment of welfare reform policies, expansion of child health coverage, and the devolution of authority and funding in many policy areas to states. (p. ix)

One outcome of this renewed interest has been the involvement of many school systems in home-visiting programs for students who are also parents of young children. Such programs often focus on helping young parents complete their education and acquire parenting skills.

## Program Effectiveness

Since the 1990s, many authors have addressed the effectiveness of home visiting. They have both reviewed the existing research and conducted meta-analyses of these studies. The reviews have shown mixed results (Daro & Harding, 1999; Greenberg et al., 2001; Guterman, 2000; Substance Abuse and Mental Health Services Administration, n.d.; Sweet & Appelbaum, 2004).

Reviews of studies on national programs that focused on increasing parenting skills to ensure children's school readiness have yielded inconsistent findings (Gomby et al., 1999; Gomby, Larson, Lewit, & Behrman, 1993). The most consistently positive outcomes have come from Nurse–Family Partnership and its earlier models (Olds et al., 1999).

However, two home-visiting programs have obtained strong empirical support for their procedures. One of these is the work of Lutzker, Bigelow, Doctor, Gershater, and Greene (1998), who developed and researched an ecobehavioral approach to address adult and child neglect, finding strong support for reducing parental behaviors associated with abuse and neglect. A second noteworthy example of an effective home-visiting program is multisystemic therapy for serious juvenile delinquents, which draws from several theories, including ecological theory, family systems theory, behavioral theory, and cognitive-behavioral theory. This home-visiting program has resulted in reduced antisocial behavior, less substance abuse, and less aggression with peers (Henggeler, Schoenwald, Borduin, Rowland, & Cunningham, 1998).

Concern with the absence of positive outcome data in some experimental studies has led to detailed analyses of process and outcome data. One exemplary analysis of Hawaii's Healthy Start program questions the adequacy of the preparation and training of the home visitors (Duggan et al., 2004). In examining why child and parent outcomes were not strong, researchers found that paraprofessional home visitors were not identifying or were failing to address several key predictors of abuse and neglect: partner violence, substance abuse, and parental depression.

These findings have important implications for school social workers and others who provide home-visiting services as they provide compelling evidence of the need to ensure that visitors are well trained and have the knowledge and skills essential to address the goals and objectives of the program. Home visitors need to be thoroughly acquainted with the basics of visiting, equipped with strong clinical and helping skills, and knowledgeable of the skills specific to the intervention that is being implemented. Furthermore, home visitors need access to professional development and ongoing supervision in order to reflect on and improve their practice.

# What We Can Do

## Home-Visiting Principles
In this section, we present principles that help in focusing the work of the home visitor, information for planning the home visit, and a framework for the home visit itself. We focus on general strategies for home visits (such as the need to engage the family in a working relationship), rather than specific interventions for particular family needs. However, numerous interventions described throughout this book can be used within the context of home visits to reach specific goals.

## Guidelines
First, as illustrated in Table 6.1, we identify guidelines that help structure the home visit. These guidelines help home visitors recognize that they are guests in the family's home and that they need to work with the family in a collaborative and flexible manner, provide individualized services, and help families to obtain resources that can help sustain changes over time.

## Preparation for the Home Visit
Preparing for a home visit may take more time than preparing to see a parent or family in an office or school setting because you must not only prepare for the content of the meeting and learn about the family but also learn about the community surrounding the home in order to gain relevant information for visiting the family. A considerable amount of preparation is essential if you have not previously visited with the family, or in the neighborhood. Specific preparation activities are listed next.

| **Table 6.1** Home-Visiting Guidelines |
| --- |

- Home visitors should view the family as a social system where changes in one individual in the family can influence other family members as well as the overall functioning of the family.
- Home-based interventions should be individualized, whether focused on a specific family member or the entire family.
- Home visitors can best conceptualize their helping relationship as a collaboration between the home visitor and the family members, which builds on the family's strengths.
- Home visitors must be flexible and responsive to the immediate needs of families as well as to their long-term goals.
- Home visitors need to continually evaluate the family's strengths, limitations, and progress and use this knowledge to modify interventions as necessary.
- Home visitors need to be able to encourage effective coping and problem-solving skills.
- Home visitors should remain attentive to the family's future needs and help the members consider ways that newly acquired skills or attitudes might be generalized to future situations.
- Home visitors need to link the family with natural helping systems in the community, resources that can support the family after services are terminated (e.g., extended family members, significant others, neighbors, clubs, and faith organizations).

*Source*: Adapted from Wasik, B. H. & Bryant, D. M. (2001). *Home visiting: Procedures for helping families* (2nd ed.). Thousand Oaks, CA: Sage.

## Learn About the Family

What is the composition of the family? Are supportive relatives or friends nearby? When are family members most likely to be at home? Who do you expect to be present in the home? Are there special considerations involved in visiting with this family? Is this a voluntary or mandated visit? If your organization or school has provided services to this family before, what knowledge can be shared with you? Such information could include which family members are most supportive of the visit or whether any difficulties have been experienced before.

## Review the Purpose of the Visit

Reflect on the goals and purposes of the visit. Think through what you hope to accomplish on the visit and what steps you think might be necessary to accomplish the goals. Ask yourself the following questions: If this is not the first visit, did you leave any adult or student informational materials during your last visit? Did you expect any tasks to be completed between the last visit and this one? Determine what materials you might need for the visit, such as school forms or records, parenting materials, or referral information.

Remember, both general and specific knowledge and skills are essential for effective home visiting. Ask yourself what specific skills and competencies are needed for this visit. For example, does a parent need to have an interpretation of a psychological report? Should the school nurse go on this home visit with you? Do you need to address the student's low school achievement? Would it be advantageous for the student's teacher to be on this visit? Did you obtain any data at the last visit that need to be considered? Is there a specific intervention protocol to be followed for this visit?

## Set the Time

Make contact with the family in advance to confirm the date and time for the visit. If this time is set up more than a few days in advance, reconfirm the day and time before the visit, if possible. This task may be difficult as families may not have phones or may be unwilling to share contact information.

## Learn the Characteristics of the Neighborhood

Learn how to get to the home. If necessary, make a trial trip to the home to ensure that you know the location. Have a map of the community and the neighborhood and use an online travel direction program to assist you in your preparations.

## Consider Personal Safety

In today's society, safety issues can occur in any neighborhood, and as previously mentioned, the majority of school social workers view home visits as potentially dangerous situations (Astor et al., 1998). Consequently, home visitors should attend to basic personal safety issues. Having a cell phone that can be used to make quick contact with others is prudent behavior, as is letting another responsible person know when and where you will be visiting and when you are expected back. Decide if the safety concerns call for you to visit during the day or with a coworker. In some instances, you may benefit from using the school resource officer as an escort (Wasik & Coleman, 2004).

## Conducting the Home Visit

The framework we present here has relevance across home visiting for many purposes related to working with children, youth, and their families (Wasik & Sparling, 1998). Each topic presented in Table 6.2 identifies one aspect of the home visit. Reviewing each of these aspects before making a home visit will help ensure that you have thoroughly thought through the overall structure of the home visit as well as have made considerations for the specific visit. Reflecting on this set of items after the home visit can help you evaluate your actions in the home and learn from the visit. Additional detailed information appears in Wasik and Sparling (1998).

In addition to the structure provided in the table, good home visits happen when the home visitor employs strong helping skills. School social workers and other mental health counselors are introduced to these during their

**Table 6.2** Aspects of Home Visits

| | Visitor's Actions and Responsibilities |
| --- | --- |
| Greeting and engagement | Greet family members warmly and establish rapport<br>Discuss purpose of home visit |
| Assessment of current family/child status | Ask about changes since last visit<br>Discuss<br>• current status of child or youth and parent/family<br>• family needs and resources |
| Child/adolescent focus | Discuss goals/objectives for the child or adolescent<br>Inquire about recent activities or services<br>Jointly plan with family for any new activities or interventions<br>Describe fully any new activities or interventions<br>Assure that family understands |
| Parent–child focus | Discuss specific parent concerns regarding child/adolescent<br>Help parent resolve difficulties in parent–child relationships<br>Jointly plan with family for any new activities or interventions<br>Assure that family understands |
| Family focus | Respond appropriately to family culture, practices, and beliefs<br>Encourage participation of family members as appropriate<br>Discuss family social support network as needed |
| Health/safety | Identify/respond to health issues<br>Make referrals as appropriate |
| Parent coping and problem solving | Use effective problem-solving strategies<br>Encourage parents to clarify concerns and problems<br>Help parents develop strategies and follow through |

*(continued)*

**Table 6.2** *(Continued)*

| | Visitor's Actions and Responsibilities |
|---|---|
| Case management and coordination | Discuss other services<br>Discuss any coordination issues<br>Make referrals as appropriate |
| Closure and planning for next steps | Recap main points of visit<br>Discuss specific goals of coming weeks<br>Provide<br>• time for parent/family input<br>• encouragement for next steps<br>Arrange for next meeting |

**Table 6.3** Clinical Interviewing Skills

Visitor communicates warmth and caring.
Visitor conveys empathy.
Visitor puts parent/family at ease.
Visitor uses a collaborative manner.
Visitor individualizes services.
Visitor listens attentively.
Visitor is reflective and thoughtful.
Visitor is appropriately directive.
Visitor questions/probes as needed.
Visitor clarifies or restates client goals or needs.
Visitor provides support and encouragement.
Visitor compliments parents and students on strengths or positive activities.
Visitor is appropriately responsive to parent or student emotions.
Visitor uses appropriate clinical techniques.

training, but it is helpful to list those that are especially important for home visits (see Table 6.3). In essence, you want to put the family at ease, be respectful and nonjudgmental, and use procedures that engage the family and help them make progress toward their own goals.

The clinical skills listed in Table 6.3 are important for engaging with families and helping them accept and address concerns. Home visitors can also benefit by using a structure, such as a problem-solving strategy, to guide their interactions related to specific concerns or issues (see Table 6.4). This strategy helps home visitors in their interactions with a family by clarifying the status or progress made in the problem-solving process and what is needed to move forward. Using a problem-solving strategy can provide greater focus to the home visit and provide more clarity to the concerns being addressed. A strategy such as this is

**Table 6.4** Problem-Solving Strategy

1. *Problem definition*: describing a problem situation (a situation is defined as a problem when its resolution is not automatic)
2. *Goal selection*: describing what a person wants to happen
3. *Generation of solutions*: identifying a number of alternative responses that may address a problem or reach a goal
4. *Consideration of consequences*: identifying the positive and negative consequences of any solution in relation to time; money; personal, emotional, and social effects; immediate and long-term effects
5. *Decision making*: weighing the proposed solutions and consequences and appropriately determining which one is best for the individual at the time (decision making includes consideration of a person's priorities and values)
6. *Implementation*: carrying out those actions called for by the decision
7. *Evaluation*: reviewing the outcome to determine whether it met the person's goals

especially helpful when you are not using a programmed or scripted intervention. Additional information on the use of this problem-solving strategy can be found in Wasik and Bryant (2001).

# Resource Bibliography: Programs Incorporating Home Visiting

For those providing home-visiting services, it is important to become familiar with specific programs and their empirical database. The resource bibliography presents a selection of specific programs that incorporate home visiting, a brief description and focus of each, selected outcomes, and contact information. Table 6.5 lists a range of home-visiting programs serving children from infancy to late adolescence and their families. This list, although just a starting point, provides the reader with information on the breadth of issues being addressed through home-visiting services and examples of the kinds of procedures that are used.

# Key Points to Remember

This chapter has provided an overview of home visiting for school social workers and others working within educational organizations. We gave some background on the advantages of home visiting and its prevalence and general guidelines to help social workers begin to practice in this setting. We also provided helpful information for review as the social worker prepares for a home visit and a

**Table 6.5** Home-Visiting Programs

| Resource | Description | Selected Outcomes | Contact |
|---|---|---|---|
| Parents as Teachers | Early childhood parent education and family support program. Focus: 0–5 years | Parents engage in language and literacy-promoting behaviors; children score high on kindergarten readiness tests | Parents as Teachers National Center www.patnc.org |
| First Steps to Success | Goal is to divert antisocial behavior in kindergarteners. Three components: universal screening, school and home intervention. Being introduced to Head Start children and families. Focus: kindergarteners | Decrease in aggression; increase in adaptive behavior and academic achievement. | Hill M. Walker, Co-Director Institute on Violence and Destructive Behavior 1265 University of Oregon, Eugene, OR 97403-1265 Phone: (541) 346-3580 E-mail: hwalker@oregon.uoregon.edu |
| Early Risers: Skills for Success | The program is specifically aimed at children who display early aggressive, disruptive, and/or nonconformist behaviors. Focus: 6–10 years | Improvement in academic achievement and social skills; decreased behavior problems | Gerald J. August, Ph.D. University of Minnesota F256/2B West 2450 Riverside Avenue Minneapolis, MN 55454-1495 Phone: (612) 273-9711 Fax: (612) 273-9779 E-mail: augus001@tc.umn.edu |
| Multisystemic Therapy | Family oriented family therapy, home-based. Focus: violent, substance-abusing youth 12–17 years | Cost-efficient reduction in substance use and antisocial behavior in serious, chronic, juvenile offenders | Scott W. Henggeler, Ph.D. Family Services Research Center, Medical University of South Carolina E-mail: Henggesw@musc.edu |

*Source:* U.S. Department of Health and Human Services, Substance Abuse and Mental Health Services Administration and the Administration for Children & Families; Program Web sites.

framework for conducting the home visit itself. In addition, we suggested a problem-solving strategy as a way of providing structure and guidance to the home-visiting process. Additional resources will need to be consulted for those new to home visiting. These resources include both general sources on home visiting and sources specific to the objectives for the home visit. Seeking out other experienced home visitors for mentoring and supervision is also a way to master the skills needed to be an effective home visitor.

# Helping Children in Foster Care and Other Residential Placements Succeed in School

*Dorian E. Traube*
*Mary M. McKay*

## Getting Started

Many children in out-of-home placements experience emotional or behavioral difficulties. Even children who do not exhibit overt symptoms are at risk for the development of mental health difficulties as a result of histories of child abuse and neglect, poverty, adult caregiver mental health concerns, stress related to removal from their families, or placement disruption (Cox, Orme, & Rhodes, 2003). Each year, billons of dollars are spent responding to the legal, correctional, educational, and psychological needs of children in out-of-home placements (Atkins et al., 1998). Yet, despite this, children residing in out-of-home placements are also seriously affected by deteriorating supportive resources, including a shortage of mental health service providers.

Schools are one of the few existing resources consistently available within communities, and they offer a unique opportunity to provide mental health care for children in the child-protective system. Among the advantages schools provide is the opportunity to intervene with a child and foster family or group home coordinator in a community setting, to enhance children's academic progress and affect children's peer relations, to increase access to underserved children via their availability in schools, and to lessen the stigma of mental health services (Atkins et al., 1998). Given the shortages of mental health resources in many communities, there is increasing awareness that schools are de facto mental health service providers for a majority of children, including those in out-of-home placements (Atkins et al., 1998).

## What We Know About the Existing School-Based Mental Health Consultation Model

The predominant model for school-based mental health services is the consultation model. In this model, mental health providers, generally social workers, consult with teachers to develop services targeting the needs of the referred student. These consultations are important elements of providing child mental health care and are supported by numerous studies identifying the effectiveness of mental health–focused interventions in schools (Axelrod, 1977; Mash & Barkley, 1989).

Though there is not sufficient space to detail all empirically driven models of best practice with children in out-of-home placement, the authors refer the readers to the following school-based mental health interventions:

### To Treat Emotional and Behavioral Disorders

Catron, T., & Weiss, B. (1994). The Vanderbilt school–based counseling program: An interagency, primary-care model of mental health services. *Journal of Emotional and Behavioral Disorders, 2,* 247–253.

Hawkins, J. D., Catalano, R. F., Kosterman, R., Abbott, R., & Hill, K. (1999). Preventing adolescent health-risk behaviors by strengthening protection during childhood. *Archives of Pediatric and Adolescent Medicine, 153,* 226–234.

### To Treat Depression

Clarke, G., Hawkins, W., Murphy, M., Sheeber, L., Lewinsohn, P., & Seeley, J. (1995). Targeted prevention of unipolar depressive disorder in an at-risk sample of high school adolescents: A randomized trial of a group cognitive intervention. *Journal of the American Academy of Child and Adolescent Psychiatry, 34,* 312–321.

### To Treat Conduct Disorders

Battistich, V., Schaps, E., Watson, M., & Solomon, D. (1996). Prevention effects of the Child Development Project: Early findings from an ongoing multisite demonstration trial. *Journal of Adolescent Research, 11,* 12–35.

See also Chapter 2. Table 7.1 describes some of the recent, innovative, empirically driven, direct intervention school mental health models that extend the reach of schools to provide for the social and emotional needs of children.

Although these school mental health models are considered advances and have substantial empirical support, many of these models and related interventions are rejected by teachers as being either too complex to be managed independently or too distinct from standard educational practices for teachers and school administrators to embrace. Furthermore, necessary financial or innovative staff resources are often not available to sustain innovative mental health service models for children. Yet, an important advantage of each of these models is that they do not specifically identify children in out-of-home placements as being in need. Since these models promote the mental health and well-being of *all* children in a school, the child in out-of-home placement is part of a supportive, stable school environment instead of being further stigmatized for needs that developed as a result of a history of abuse or neglect.

**Table 7.1** Innovative School-Based Mental Health Services

*Program: Success for All*

*Author:* Robert Slavin, Nancy Karweit, Barbara Wasik

*Description:*

**Elements:** Combines quality day care, academic tutoring, and parent support service.

**Goal:** To prevent academic problems by providing quality early childhood education, remediate academic deficits, provide parents with education about health.

*Obtaining More Information:* Book: *Preventing early failure: research, policy, and practice.*

---

*Program: School of the 21st Century*

*Author:* Edward Zigler

*Description:*

**Elements:** Attracts noncompulsory parent participation, avoids deficit-based mentality of traditional mental health services.

**Goal:** To increase mother–child interactions, stabilize child-care arrangements, improve academic outcomes.

*Obtaining More Information:* Addressing the nation's childcare crises: The school of the 21st century, *American Journal of Orthopsychiatry* 59(1989), 485–491.

---

*Program: School Development Program*

*Author :* James Comer, Norris Haynes, Edward Joyner, Michael Ben-Avie

*Description:*

**Elements:** Modifies school climate by enhancing the relations among school staff, students, and parents in urban low-income schools.

**Goal:** To increase academic gains, reduce suspensions, reduce corporal punishment, increase parent involvement.

*Obtaining More Information:* Book: Rallying the whole village: *The Comer process for reforming education.*

---

*Program: Constructie Discipline*

*Author:* Greta Mayer

*Description:*

**Elements:** Provides clearly stated rules for child, consistent enforcement of rules, planned rewards for appropriate behavior, staff support.

**Goal:** to reduce antisocial behavior, create a positive school climate.

*Obtaining More Information:* Preventing Antisocial Behavior in School, *Journal of Applied Behavioral Analysis,* 28(1989), 467–478.

# What We Can Do—Parents and Peers as Leaders in School Approach

Another example of an innovation in the field of school-based practice has grown out of an increasing realization that childhood mental health disorders are affected by numerous factors beyond the level of the child. However, few school-based models have considered the specific, complex interactions of the multiple factors affecting children being reared in out-of-home placements. The Parents and Peers as Leaders in School (PALS) approach offers an innovative, ecological model guiding school-based mental health care, and it is a potential resource for youth in out-of-home placements. PALS, developed by Atkins, McKay, Abdul-Adil, and colleagues at the University of Illinois at Chicago, is intended to provide individualized, flexible, and coordinated mental health services for youth within their school settings. It targets children and adolescents who might not be successfully involved in care because of a shortage of providers, stigma associated with receipt of care, or mobility. For children in out-of-home placements, these barriers to mental health care abound. Therefore, there is an excellent opportunity for goodness-of-fit between the PALS school-based service delivery model and the needs of children in out-of-home placement.

## Premises of the Parents and Peers as Leaders in School Service Delivery Model

The PALS model proposes that empirically based strategies, including multisystemic therapy, are available to reduce child mental health difficulties across the multiple ecologies of schools: at the school level (e.g., providing appropriate and engaging classroom activities), at the peer level (e.g., providing appropriate teacher and peer models for classroom activities), at the adult caregiver level (e.g., involving adult caregivers in the child's educational and behavioral goals at school), and at the child level (e.g., social skills). For more information on these empirically based strategies, see Atkins et al. (1998, 2001, 2003a, 2003b). The PALS model is flexible and individualized by acknowledging that contexts for child mental health will differ across children and by providing services specific to those contexts. This flexibility is particularly relevant to children in out-of-home placements because their needs will vary according to their history and current placement status.

## Goals of Parents and Peers as Leaders in School

PALS seeks to improve all children's learning experiences by

1. helping children manage their behavior at school and at home,
2. supporting children in the classroom,

3. supporting schools in planning for children's long-term needs,
4. supporting teachers in promoting positive classroom behavior and improving learning within their classroom,
5. increasing adult caregiver involvement in the child's education,
6. assisting adult caregivers in developing necessary resources for children to succeed at school,
7. offering practical ideas to adult caregivers on how to manage the children's needs,
8. supporting adult caregivers in linking to community resources, and
9. supporting adult caregiver and teacher collaboration to improve classroom behavior and learning.

Because children spend the vast majority of their time in school, coordination between schools and care providers boost the chances that the needs of children in out-of-home placements will be attended to in a systematic and synchronized way.

## Parents and Peers as Leaders in School Systematic Assessment

A key feature of the PALS model is to identify settings in which mental health issues emerge for the child throughout the school day. Once these settings have been identified, they are targeted using a social learning theory perspective. Social learning theory guides social workers to focus on

- the degree to which students are supervised or *monitored,*
- the extent to which students are *motivated* to behave appropriately, and
- the extent to which prosocial alternatives and social support are *modeled* by peers and adults.

The goal of PALS is to identify the level at which social learning principles are applicable and the degree to which factors within the school environment can be modified. For children in out-of-home placements, social learning theory provides a platform for transferable skills that they can apply within and outside the school environment.

## Establishing Collaborative Working Relationships

The PALS model emphasizes the need for systematic assessment of child mental health difficulties and identifies factors that contribute to these at school and in the after-school environment. The model also specifies the need to involve teachers and adult caregivers in the systematic assessment of intervention needs. As previously noted, the goal of this assessment is to target problems and potential solutions using a social learning model approach (modeling, motivation, and monitoring). The PALS social worker brings to this collaboration a range of empirically validated interventions. Teachers and adult caregivers bring the practical realities of schools and foster families and/or residential treatment environments. It is this collaborative group that develops a menu of options specific to each child and his or her classroom's needs with the goal of intervening at multiple levels of the school ecology simultaneously (e.g., increasing student motivation, increasing teacher monitoring) and at the family/residential context (e.g., availability of homework help after school, increasing foster adult caregiver involvement in school supportive activities). However, the single most important theme in PALS is that instead of targeting individual children, PALS offers services that affect the *whole* classroom and extend to contexts after school. PALS aims to increase positive attitudes and behaviors among *all* children in a classroom and gives all children the opportunity for academic and social success. It is the premise of the PALS model that every teacher, classroom, and out-of-home placement has unique strengths and needs that could be overlooked by focusing on individual children. Potentially, focusing on the entire classroom creates a supportive environment for the foster child rather than further stigmatizing him or her via removal from class for individual sessions.

## Steps in Conducting Parents and Peers as Leaders in School Assessments
### Foster Family Assessments
Once a child has been referred to PALS, it is necessary to complete two levels of assessments. The first level is a family/environmental assessment. Because the child is currently in foster care, it is necessary to speak directly to the foster care agency representing the child. The agency should be able to offer information about the child's social, emotional, and family history, including any auxiliary services the child may be receiving from the agency (e.g., supervised visits with the birth family, tutoring, medical care). The foster care agency will have to supply the worker with written consent to interview the child because it serves as the child's legal guardian.

After the worker receives consent to assess the child, he or she should proceed by contacting the foster family or residential facility staff to explain the PALS program and to request a meeting with them. In addition, we advise that the worker make a visit to the foster or group home to assess the environment in which the child currently lives. Because children who have been removed from their biological family have had major disruptions in their lives, the PALS social worker should pay attention to elements of the environment that may contribute to further life disruptions, including poor supervision, chaotic daily schedules, and adult caregivers unable to know what is occurring while the child is out of the home. The environmental assessment allows the PALS team to identify and address situations in the foster child's life that may contribute to academic and social difficulties.

## Classroom Assessment

The next step in implementing PALS involves assessing the classroom of the foster child. Because PALS will be implemented for the entire class, it is important to determine how the class is currently operating. The following list has some key assumptions to remember when visiting classrooms.

- Every classroom has strengths and needs; identification of needs without considering strengths provides a distorted view of the classroom.
- The team will always demonstrate respect for the teachers' roles and responsibilities and appreciation for the teachers' knowledge and ability to manage the classroom.
- Assessment is ongoing and continuous; it starts from the moment the team begins to meet and continues throughout the team's time together.

Initially, the assessment can be "informal," which involves the PALS social worker or counselor acting as a *participant observer* in the classroom. Formal assessment does not differ from the steps outlined earlier, but more specific information is gathered, such as

- times of day that are especially difficult and times of day when things tend to run smoothly,
- activities of the day that are especially difficult and those that run smoothly,
- student's activities during these times/activities,
- teacher's activities and responsibilities during these times/activities,
- other adults who may be present during these times/activities,
- whether or not things ever run differently, and if they do, what is happening during those atypical times.

A comprehensive assessment creates the basis for developing an intervention plan that best addresses the multiple needs of the child in out-of-home placement. The assessment of the classroom allows the PALS team to determine the times and situations where intervention can occur on behalf of the foster child to create a supportive environment. This supportive environment is thought to serve as a corrective experience for children who may have rarely experienced such support.

## Parents and Peers as Leaders in School Intervention

Once the assessments have been completed and appropriate goals have been established for the child, intervention can be begun. At this stage there will be two levels of intervention—one with the adult caregivers and one within the classroom.

## Intervention With the Adult Caregiver

PALS adult caregiver goals are hierarchical. In other words, PALS focuses first on the primary goal, that is, adult caregiver's involvement in the child's education, then the second goal, that is, increasing adult caregivers' social support. Finally, the third goal is to assist adult caregivers in building and developing their skills to care for children. These adult caregivers' goals were developed with the belief that if adult caregivers are more involved in their children's education, feel supported, and have skills, they will be better able to support the childern's learning and mental health. The two lists are provided here, one for foster parents and one for group home workers that can be provided to help them develop their involvement skills.

*Ways Foster Parents Can Support a Positive Learning Environment*

- Ask the child what happened at school that day, and listen to the response.
- Always be respectful of the child's teacher in the child's presence.
- Meet with the teacher if the child is having behavior problems to discuss appropriate consequences at home and in school.
- Respond promptly to notes and phone calls from school.
- Attend adult caregiver/teacher conferences, report card pickup day, and as many other school events as possible.
- Request meetings with teachers to discuss the child's progress, especially when problems are not occurring.

*Ways for Group Home Workers to Support a Child's Education*
*at the Residential Placement*

- Supervise homework. Provide a quiet place for the child to work. Turn off the TV, do not talk on the phone unless absolutely necessary, and ask visitors to return another time, if possible.
- Check child's school bag daily for necessary school supplies and homework.
- Give reasonable rewards for good work and good behavior.
- Establish a school–home report.
- Build a positive relationship with the foster child: engage in fun activities with him or her.

This support is vital to ensuring academic and mental health success because the adult caregiver will be a stabilizing force for a child who has experienced major instability throughout his or her life.

## Intervention at the Classroom Level

As mentioned earlier, the PALS classroom goals are interconnected. PALS goals were developed with the assumption that if the classroom is organized and the students are academically engaged and feel supported, then behavioral problems will decrease, and academic success will increase. Some proposed strategies to achieve the PALS classroom goals are listed here.

*Strategies for Increasing Academic Engagement*

- Discuss with the teacher the assumption that students who are engaged academically learn more and have fewer behavioral problems. Teachers are all different, and the goal is not to tell the teacher how to teach. On the other hand, research has demonstrated that children are more academically engaged when lessons are interesting and the teacher's presentation is animated. Encourage teachers to be creative when presenting new information.
- Encourage teachers to give clear instructions (e.g., write them on the board or repeat them several times) and examples to illustrate what should be learned.

*Strategies for Improving Classroom Organization*

- Review with teachers that a well-organized class can lead to a well-behaved class.
- Encourage teachers to establish rules for in-class and out-of-class behavior and to communicate clearly well-defined consequences of breaking the rules.
- Emphasize to teachers that they need to enforce the rules and stick to the consequences.
- Encourage teachers to review the rules with the class on a regular basis, especially after a violation has occurred.
- Encourage teachers to keep an organized desk and clean classroom. They can provide an example for the children to follow regarding their own desk and books.

Deciding on a classroom intervention should be based on the information gathered during the PALS practitioner's classroom observations and the teacher's needs assessment. The PALS school-based professional will generate a list of possible interventions that address the classroom needs identified during the assessment phase. Once identified, the interventions are reviewed with the classroom teacher. Thus, each PALS classroom will have its own unique treatment plan.

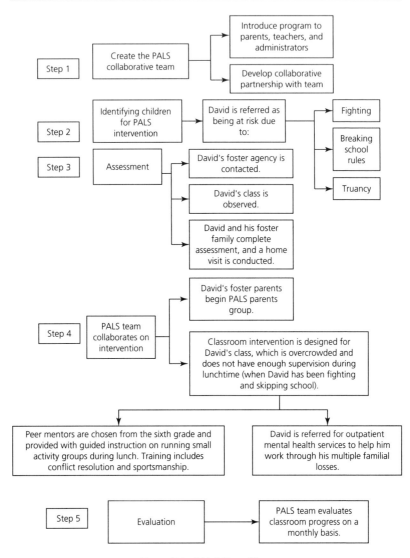

**Figure 7.1.** PALS Flow Chart.

# Tools and Practice Examples

David is a 10-year-old foster child residing in a low-income urban neighborhood. His mother lost custody of him when he was 5 years old because of her drug addiction. Last year she passed away from a drug overdose. David was placed for a year and a half with a foster family in his neighborhood. However, his mother's sister requested custody of him, and the courts decided kinship foster care was the more appropriate living arrangement. David's aunt decided 6 months later that David was too difficult to control and asked that he be removed from her custody. Over the last 3 years, David has been in five different kinship foster homes and lived in four different neighborhoods. He currently lives with his mother's cousin and her three children. He has been skipping school, picking fights in his 5th-grade class, and disobeying school rules.

Figure 7.1 shows the steps for implementing the PALS model.

## Resources

Fantuzzo, J. W., & Atkins, M. S. (1992). Applied behavior analysis for educators: Teacher centered and classroom based. *Journal of Applied Analysis, 25,* 35–42.

Holtzman, W. H. (1992), *School of the future.* Washington, DC: American Psychological Association.

Lynn, C. J., McKay, M. M., & Atkins, M. S. (2003). School social work: Meeting the mental health needs of students through collaboration with teachers. *Children and School, 25*(4), 197–209.

McKay, M. M., Gonzales, J., Quintana, E., Kim, L., & Abdul-Adil, J. (1999). Multiple family groups: An alternative for reducing disruptive behavioral difficulties of urban children. *Research on Social Work Practice, 9*(5), 593–607.

McKay, M. M., Harrison, M. E., Gonzales, J., Kim, L., & Quintana, E. (2002). Multiple-family groups for urban children with conduct difficulties and their families. *Psychiatric Services, 53*(11), 1467–1468.

Peters, B. R., Atkins, M. S., & McKay, M. M. (1999). Adopted children's behavior problems: A review of five explanatory models. *Clinical Psychology Review, 19*(3), 297–328.

Tolan, P. H., Hanish, L. D., McKay, M. M., & Dickey, M. H. (2002). Evaluating process in child and family interventions: Aggression prevention as an example. *Journal of Family Psychology, 16*(2), 220–236.

# Key Points to Remember

- Children living in out-of-home placements have historically been affected by high rates of community violence, poverty, and substance abuse; deteriorating support resources; and a serious shortage of mental health services.
- It is important to develop effective mental health services for urban children that attend to these environmental influences.

- To this end, schools offer a unique environment for helping children and families in low-income communities.
- Through schools, service providers are able to reach large numbers of traditionally underserved children and to interact with children and adult caregivers.
- The PALS program was developed as an alternative to existing service delivery models in clinics and in schools.
- PALS addresses the limitations of clinic-based consultation and school-based health clinics by (a) working directly with teachers to establish interventions that are tailored to the needs of individual teachers and classrooms and (b) involving adult caregivers in their child's education in an effort to enhance children's learning.
- It is the belief of the PALS program that classrooms have unique strengths to offer support and continued growth for children in out-of-home placements.

# Primary Prevention of Pregnancy

**8**

## Effective School-Based Programs

*Mary Beth Harris*

## Getting Started

For decades the educational, social, and economic consequences of adolescent pregnancy and childbirth have presented a compelling challenge to schools. High schools and middle schools were coping with the growing presence of teen pregnancy for more than 15 years before it caught the country's attention in the 1980s. Between 1972 and 1990 births to teenage mothers increased by 27% to an all-time high (National Campaign to Prevent Teen Pregnancy, 2004).

These numbers alone were alarming to educators and health care professionals, but it was the continuing rise in nonmarital births and welfare dependency among adolescent mothers that placed teen pregnancy at the center of legislative debate and national program initiatives. Thus began a national focus on preventing adolescent pregnancy, fueled early on with relatively small grants and later with $250 million for abstinence education programs provided by the 1996 Welfare Reform Law. By 2001 more than 700 public-funded pregnancy prevention programs had been established in over 47% of urban communities across the United States, in community agencies and churches, medical facilities, and schools (Jindal, 2001).

Most experts agree that the reduction in the national adolescent birthrate between 1991 and 2000 was likely the result of several factors, including not only more sex education and pregnancy prevention programs but also growing concern about HIV and STD, and a decade of widespread financial well-being that provided youth with more life opportunities. Statistics cited in a recent report from the Alan Guttmacher Institute (2004) showed that in 2000 the birthrate for adolescent women aged 15–17 was 29% lower than that in 1991. Birthrates declined most for African American women (31%) and least for Hispanic adolescents (15%) (Alan Guttmacher Institute, 2004). This report also indicates that the birthrate for younger adolescents, who are believed to be the most at risk for negative consequences, has remained at 0.9% per 1,000. Even with these indications of progress, however, there are 820,000 teen pregnancies each year, and over 400,000 teen births (National Campaign to Prevent Teen Pregnancy, 2004). Nearly 4 out of 10 adolescent girls in this country get pregnant at least once before they reach the age of 20. This is a higher adolescent pregnancy rate, by far, than in any other industrialized nation (Singh & Darroch, 2000).

With teen pregnancy still an issue of deep concern, schools often depend on mental health staff to provide pregnancy prevention services. Programs numbering in the hundreds can be overwhelming to school-based practitioners who have the responsibility to select a program that is effective and that fits with the school and the local community. Teen pregnancy and sex education remain controversial "hot topics," and programs vary in emphasis and content. When social workers and mental health services are competing for school and community resources, selecting or developing a pregnancy prevention program that demonstrates visible results is a priority.

This chapter explores school-based pregnancy prevention practices and programs currently in use in schools across the nation. It identifies programs and program components that have been evaluated and demonstrated to be effective in modifying adolescent sexual behavior and preventing adolescent pregnancy. It provides guidance for assessing program goodness-of-fit to the needs and values of the local school and community, and for planning and carrying out programs demonstrated effective in school settings. A bibliography of resources provides program specifics and contact information for locating programs that have been demonstrated to be effective.

## What We Know

On a daily basis school-based mental health professionals witness the discouraging consequences of adolescent pregnancy for teenage parents and their children. Even though the national rate of adolescent pregnancy has diminished in the United States, the problem is still very real and present in American schools. At the forefront of concerns is the phenomenally high rate of school dropouts among adolescent mothers. Across the nation, more than 60% of teen mothers who have a child before the age of 18 drop out of high school (National Campaign to Prevent Teen Pregnancy, 2002).

Not completing high school or a General Educational Development (GED) by the age of 20 is a heavy indicator of future poverty. Women who become mothers in adolescence, along with their children, are far more likely to live in poverty than women who postpone childbearing until their twenties. According to a National Campaign to Prevent Teen Pregnancy Fact Sheet (2002), virtually all of the increase in child poverty over the last two decades was related to the increase in nonmarital childbearing, half of which was related to mothers who had their first child in their teens. About 51% of all mothers on welfare had their first child as a teenager. About one fourth of teen mothers have a second child within 24 months of the first birth, further contributing to economic dependency and poverty (National Campaign to Prevent Teen Pregnancy, 2002).

The penalties for children born to teenage mothers are numerous and serious. They are more likely to be born prematurely and be of low birth weight, leading to a number of chronic medical and developmental problems. They are 50% more likely to fall behind academically and less likely to graduate from high school (Haeman, Wolfe, & Peterson, 1997). Sons are 13% more likely to become involved with the law and to be incarcerated (Haeman et al., 1997). Daughters are 22% more likely to become teen mothers themselves (Terry & Manlove, 2000). They are more likely to be poor. These children are more restricted by developmental, economic, and social factors that limit their resources and life options than children born to mothers aged 20 and older.

# What We Can Do

Over the last two decades the number of adolescent pregnancy prevention programs has mushroomed into the hundreds, some focused on primary prevention and others on preventing subsequent pregnancies (Franklin & Corcoran, 2000). In this chapter we review programs in which the main goal is to prevent first-time pregnancies.

## Program Categories and Emphasis

Pregnancy prevention programs can be categorized according to their distinctive features and special emphases. This chapter is concerned with school-based and school-linked programs where the school system takes primary responsibility. It is also helpful for school-based practitioners to be familiar with local community programs offered at social service agencies or in hospitals or clinics. The format and focus of programs that have been evaluated and demonstrated as effective in changing sexual behavior and preventing pregnancy fall into three broad categories: (1) sex education with or without contraception, (2) youth development or life options programs, and (3) service learning programs (Manlove et al., 2004). Abstinence-only program goals can be found in all three of these categories, as well as program goals for reducing sexual behavior or risks related to sexual behavior. Another important distinction is whether *skills building* is a central goal of the program (Franklin & Corcoran, 2000). Skills building has become an especially important component in the success of prevention programs, as discussed in the next sections.

## Sex Education Programs

These programs focus on delaying (abstinence) or reducing sexual activity. They range from short courses of fewer than 10 hours to comprehensive courses of more than 40 hours. The focus of sex education prevention programs varies. Some programs include contraceptive information and distribution, while others exclude this content. Although a survey of school-based health clinics in the mid-1990s indicated that states and school districts are becoming more comfortable with programs that include contraception knowledge building (Schlitt et al., 1994), this can still be a controversial issue and should be researched in the local district before selecting a program. Regardless of contraception as a program feature, most sex education prevention programs contain these components:

1. Skills building, including decision making, interpersonal, and assertiveness
2. Values clarification
3. Relevant information provision
4. Peer education where teens can educate other teens
5. Youth theater projects where dramatic scenarios serve as catalysts for discussion
6. Computer-assisted instruction for parents and adolescents
7. Day-long conferences and training

## Life Options/Youth Development Programs

Life options programs focus on changing sexual behaviors and reducing pregnancies through enhancing life skills and increasing options for disadvantaged youths (Philliber & Allen, 1992). The core assumption, based on research evidence (Afexentiou & Hawley, 1997; Allen, Philliber, Herrling, & Kuperminc, 1997), is that youths who have higher educational aspirations and greater opportunities are more likely to delay sexual intercourse and childbearing. Life options programs target teenagers' educational and earnings opportunities, such as postsecondary education, job training programs, and guaranteed student loans.

Youth development programs with a number of components that target both sexuality and youth development are demonstrated in a number of program evaluation studies to be the most effective interventions for pregnancy prevention (Kirby, 2001). For example, the Carrera Program, a multicomponent program offered by the Children's Aid Society, was demonstrated to prevent pregnancies for as long as 3 years. This program includes interventions common to many youth development/life options programs that focus on sexuality as well as youth development, offered in combination over time. The core components of the Carrera Program are (1) family life and sex education, (2) individual academic assessment and preparation for standardized tests and college prep exams, (3) tutoring, (4) self-expression activities through use of the arts, and (5) comprehensive health and mental health care (Manlove et al., 2004).

Most effective life options programs, such as the Carrera Program (Philliber, Williams Kaye, Herrling, & West, 2002) and the Quantum Opportunities Program (Taggart & Lattimore, 2001), include sexuality and sexual behavior as a focus. Skills building in all life domains, however, is the primary curricular theme.

Here are some of the personal and social skills included in the developmental curriculum of the Quantum Opportunities Program (Manlove et al., 2004):

- Awareness skills focusing on building self-esteem, including strategies for coping with peer pressure, stereotyping, and prejudice
- Community skills, including how to use available resources such as public transportation, libraries, and clinics
- Decision-making skills focusing on issues such as dropping out of school, marriage, parenting, and attending college
- Health skills, including first aid and preventive care
- Relationship skills that help with communication abilities
- Safety skills, including discussions of risky behaviors related to alcohol, drugs, and sex

Target populations for youth development programs are male and female multiracial junior high and high school students, similar to target populations for other pregnancy prevention programs. A number of research studies have examined the effectiveness of life options/youth development programs in preventing pregnancy (e.g., Allen et al., 1997; Philliber, Williams Kaye, & Herrling, 2002), and the results are promising.

## Service Learning Programs

Service learning is generally defined as curriculum-based community service that integrates classroom learning with community service activities (Denner, Coyle, Robin, & Banspach, 2005). As prevention programs that focus on positive decision making and enhanced self-awareness and self-worth rather than directly on sexuality, service learning programs show a great deal of promise. Programs that have been evaluated, such as the Teen Outreach Program (Philliber & Allen, 1992) and the Learn and Serve America Program (Melchoir, 1998), were found to be effective in preventing pregnancy as well as other positive effects such as educational achievement and social attitudes and behavior. These programs require youth to volunteer in the community and to participate in journaling, group reflections, and classroom activities and discussions. Usually service learning is differentiated from community service alone in that service learning is organized in relation to a class with clearly stated objectives and classroom goals (Franklin & Corcoran, 2000). Across school districts service learning is the central intervention with a number of youth populations and prevention programs, such as dropout prevention and gang intervention and prevention.

These are the primary program components of the Teen Outreach Program:

- *Supervised volunteering.* Students research agencies and services and select a volunteer opportunity in the community, such as peer tutoring or volunteering in a nursing home or hospital. Throughout the year they meet regularly with their volunteer supervisor and/or classroom facilitator around their experiences.

- *Weekly classroom discussions and activities.* Students share their volunteer experiences with one another, and lessons from the accompanying curriculum *Changing Scenes* are used to focus the discussion.

A classroom curriculum, *Changing Scenes*, is used throughout the program. These are some of the topics and lessons:

- A chapter on values includes a discussion in which students explore how they learn values and an activity that engages participants in exploring their beliefs about gender roles
- A chapter on relationships includes exercises and activities on making friends, romantic relationships, the difference between love and infatuation, and dealing with pressure in relationships
- A chapter on short-term and long-term personal goals includes activities on setting and achieving goals and looking at teen parenthood and some of the barriers it poses to achieving one's life goals

## Characteristics of Effective Curriculum-Based Programs

We now recognize that effective programs exist in all three of the approaches and categories just discussed. Researcher–author Douglas Kirby (2001) identified characteristics of effective curriculum-based programs across all categories. These are common characteristics in programs that have been rigorously evaluated and found to increase the age of first sex, improve the use of contraception among sexually active teens, and/or actually reduce teen pregnancy. The following is a summary:

- They have a specific, narrow focus on *behavior,* such as delaying first sex or using contraception or condoms.
- They have theoretical approaches, such as cognitive behavior and planned behavior, that have been effective with other high-risk health-related behavior. These seek to impact the beliefs, attitudes, confidence, and skills that relate to sexual behavior, which may lead to voluntary change in sexual or contraceptive behavior.
- They give the clear message about sex and protection against STD that not having sex or using condoms or other contraception is the *right* thing to do, more than simply laying out the pros and cons of sexual choices.
- They provide basic, not detailed, information about contraception and unprotected sex.
- They address peer pressure related to sex and discuss misperceptions and "lines."

- They teach communication, negotiation, and refusal skills. Some provide clear scripts for role-playing situations on these issues.
- They include games, role playing, written exercises, videos, and small group discussions, all to help participants personalize the material. Some use peer facilitators and videos of people the students can identify with.
- They reflect the age, sexual experience, and culture of the youth participating. For example, curriculum for middle school adolescents focuses on postponing sexual intercourse, while for high schoolers, programs usually emphasize avoiding unprotected sex with abstinence or the use of contraception.
- The most effective programs last at least 14 hours or longer and have a greater number of different activities for participants.
- They are strident in carefully selecting leaders who believe in the program, and they provide leaders with training sessions that last from 6 hours to 3 days and include both information and practice in using the strategies and exercises in the curriculum.

## Tools and Practice Examples

### Effective Programs Lists

Research determining the effectiveness of pregnancy prevention programs continues to accumulate. This section focuses on lists of programs that have been rigorously evaluated and found to be effective, compiled by four recognized groups associated with adolescent pregnancy and other youth-related issues (Solomon & Card, 2004). The programs included in these lists are believed to be credible because they are based on actual behavior changes among teens in a program compared to a group of similar youth who were not in the program. Because the groups used slightly different criteria for selecting effective programs, the lists are somewhat diverse. Some programs, however, were selected for inclusion in three or all four lists. This section includes a brief discussion of criteria considered in selecting programs for each list, as well as a list of nine programs (Table 8.1) that were included in at least three of the four lists (Solomon & Card, 2004).

- *The Kirby List* (Kirby, 2001). The programs included in this list met six key criteria: (1) The program outcome was the reduction of primary pregnancy and/or STD/HIV infection, (2) the primary target population was aged 18 and younger, (3) the evaluation study used an experimental or quasi-experimental design, (4) the evaluation study had a sample of at least 100 in the combined treatment and comparison groups, (5) the evaluation study

**Table 8.1** Programs Included in at Least Three Effective Program Lists

| Name of Program | Kirby (2001) | Child Trends (2001, 2002) | PASHA Advocates (2002) | Advocates (2003) |
|---|---|---|---|---|
| *Sex Education Approach* | | | | |
| Be Proud! Be Responsible! | | * | * | * |
| Becoming a Responsible Teen | * | * | * | * |
| Making a Difference: An Abstinence Approach to STD, Teen Pregnancy, and HIV/AIDS Prevention | * | | * | * |
| Making Proud Choices | * | * | * | * |
| Reducing the Risk | * | * | | * |
| Safer Choices | * | * | * | * |
| *Service Learning Approach* | | | | |
| Reach for Health Community Youth Sources | | | | |
| Teen Outreach Program | * | * | * | * |
| *Sex Education + Youth Development Approach* | * | * | | * |
| Children's Aid Society— Carrera Program | * | * | * | * |

*Source:* Adapted from Solomon & Card, 2004.

used outcome measures of behavior or health status (in addition or instead of attitude/knowledge outcome measures), and (6) appropriate statistical analysis was used in the evaluation study.

- *The Child Trends List* (Manlove et al., & Ryan, 2001, 2002). Studies were reviewed that focused on primary pregnancy, secondary pregnancy, and/or STD/HIV prevention. Criteria included (1) a sample of youth of any age (no sample size restriction identified) and (2) evaluations with experimental design and reproductive health outcomes. Selected studies were required to measure outcomes during adolescence, regardless of whether the sample included adolescents or younger children.

- *The PASHA List 2002* (Solomon & Card, 2004; Card, Niego, Mallari, & Farrell, 1996). The PASHA list is updated on an ongoing basis, most recently in 2002. Replication kits containing materials needed to operate and evaluate 28 programs on the list are available to practitioners through PASHA (see Bibliography of Resources in this chapter). To be considered for this list, a program must target youth aged 10–19, although STD/HIV prevention programs targeting college students are also eligible. Evaluation criteria include an experimental or quasi-experimental design and pretest and posttest assessments. A follow-up period of at least 6 months is required for pregnancy prevention programs. Program outcomes criteria include delay of initiation of intercourse, frequency of intercourse, number of sexual partners, contraceptive use, refusal or negotiation skills, values, and attitudes toward risk-taking behavior.

- *The Advocates List* (Advocates for Youth, 2003). This list of 19 programs is part of a report published by Advocates for Youth, entitled *Science and Success: Sex Education and Other Programs That Work to Prevent Teen Pregnancy.* The list includes only programs that focus on primary pregnancies and STD/HIV infection. Programs included for consideration meet these criteria: (1) target youth ranging from infancy to the teen years, (2) evaluation criteria include an experimental or quasi-experimental design with treatment and control/comparison conditions, (3) a sample of at least 100 combined in treatment and control/comparison groups, (4) evaluation results must have been published in a peer-reviewed journal as a proxy for high-quality design and analysis, (5) programs must have had follow-up measures at least 3 months after completion of the intervention, and (6) programs must have had results in which two risky sexual behaviors showed significant positive change or demonstrated a significant reduction in pregnancy and/or STD/HIV rates.

## Selecting a Program and Getting Started

School mental health practitioners know that simply having been demonstrated effective is not enough if a program does not fit the school, the community, and the target population of students. At the same time, altering the goals or content of an established and effective program in order to make it fit the needs of the local school is likely to diminish the program's effectiveness. These tips can help guide the search for the best program for your particular school and community (Solomon & Card, 2004):

1. Talk with community members such as teachers, parents, local clergy and politicians, health care providers, and students, who have an

investment in the program. Enquire about their preferences and values around teen pregnancy prevention, including their views on sex education and contraception. Use what you learn from these stakeholders to aim for programs that have been found effective in achieving *goals and objectives that are relevant and acceptable* to your school and community.

2. Engage with your school's administrators and interdisciplinary mental health team about initiating a prevention program, so that all of you have investment in its operation and success. Of prime consideration is the availability of resources such as space, staff, and especially funding.

3. Look for programs that were effective with youth who are as similar to your target group of students as possible. Some important characteristics are age, gender, ethnicity, acculturation, language, incarceration status, drug and alcohol use, and literacy level. All of these can influence participants' interest in the program and ability to benefit from it.

4. Once you have narrowed your program selections to two or three, determine which of these has replication kits or treatment manuals. It is far more difficult to present a program if the original program materials are not available in a user-friendly format. PASHA (http:// www.socio. com/pasha.htm), for example, offers replication kits for 28 different programs and provides sources for nine additional programs that it identifies as effective.

## Bibliography of Resources

*Becoming a Responsible Teen*
Curriculum & materials contact: Doug Kirby, Ph.D., Senior Research Scientist
4 Carbonero Way
Scotts Valley, CA 95066
Phone: 800-435-8433
Fax: 800-435-8433
E-mail: dougk@etr.org
http://www.etr.org

*Be Proud! Be Responsible!*
Curriculum & materials contact: Select Media Film Library, 22-D
Hollywood Avenue
Hohokus, NJ 07423
Phone: 800-343-3540

Fax: 201-652-1973

http://www.selectmedia.org

*Making a Difference! An Abstinence-Based Approach to HIV/STD and Teen Pregnancy Prevention*

Curriculum and materials contact: Select Media Film Library, 22-D

Hollywood Avenue

Hohokus, NJ 07423

Phone: 800-343-5540

Fax: 201-652-1973

http://www.selectmedia.org

*Making Proud Choices*

Curriculum and materials contact: Select Media Film Library, 22-D

Hollywood Avenue

Hohokus, NJ 07423

Phone: 800-343-5540

Fax: 201-652-1973

http://www.selectmedia.org

*Children's Aid Society—Carrera Program*

Curriculum and materials contact: Michael Carrera, Ed.D.,
    Program Designer

The Children's Aid Society

105 East 22nd Street

New York, NY 10010

Phone: 212-876-9716

http://www.stopteenpregnancy.com

*Teen Outreach Program*

Program contact: Gayle Waden, TOP National Coordinator

One Greenway Plaza, Suite 550

Houston, TX 77046-0103

Phone: 713-627-2322

Fax: 713-627-3006

E-mail: gwaden@cornerstone.to

www.cornerstone.to

Note: Profiles of these and other programs, including goals, population, program size and duration, and curriculum, can be accessed on the Web site of the National Campaign to Prevent Teen Pregnancy (http://www.teenpregnancy.org).

## Key Points to Remember

Although the United States has achieved a large reduction over the last decade, adolescent pregnancy and childbirth still looms large as a complex challenge for schools dealing with young parents. Teen pregnancy prevention programs are now available in nearly half of all American urban communities, with a large number in public schools. School-based mental health practitioners are often responsible for originating, selecting, and managing teen pregnancy prevention programs and services for students at risk in their schools. Fortunately, a substantial number of diverse programs have now been rigorously evaluated and found to be effective in postponing or diminishing adolescent sexual activity and pregnancy. Practitioners with the responsibility of selecting and establishing pregnancy prevention services in the school have many choices of effective programs that fit the needs, values, and resources of their school and community. This chapter has described three approaches to teen pregnancy prevention programs, including (1) curriculum-based sex education, (2) the youth development/life options approach, and (3) the service learning approach, with program examples of each approach.

# 9

# Best School-Based Practices With Adolescent Parents

*Mary Beth Harris*

## Getting Started

Despite the good news that teen pregnancy declined steadily during the 1990s, the fact remains that 34% of girls in the United States become pregnant at least once before they reach the age of 20 (National Campaign to Prevent Teen Pregnancy, 2004). Of these adolescents, more than 400,000 give birth every year (Henshaw, 2004). At some point, most of these young women are students in public schools, where school-based professionals face the daunting challenge of keeping them in school and helping them navigate the heavy responsibilities of premature parenthood. These are some of the factors that make teen parents one of the most at-risk populations among American youth:

- They are significantly at risk for school dropout, with a dropout rate of 60% (National Campaign to Prevent Teen Pregnancy, 2002).
- They are more likely to become isolated and to be clinically depressed (Kalil, Spencer, Spieker, & Gilchrist, 1998).
- They are more likely than older mothers to have complications during pregnancy and less likely to receive prenatal care.
- Their children are significantly at risk for low birth weight, prematurity, developmental problems, insufficient health care, and school failure (Brooks-Gunn & Furstenberg, 1986; Maynard, 1997).
- They are likely to have family conflicts that limit support from their parents and the father or mother of their baby (Rhodes & Woods, 1995).
- As adults, they are more likely to live in poverty (Maynard, 1997; Moore et al., 1993).

Recent public policies such as Temporary Assistance for Needy Families (TANF) have restricted economic subsidies and services for mothers and children, creating further difficulties for this vulnerable population. Young mothers who formerly depended on public assistance and social services to help them transition into adulthood and secure postsecondary education or career training are now likely to have exhausted these benefits before they leave high school. Thus, preparing young parents for immediate and long-term economic self-sufficiency has become a critical task for school-based programs.

This chapter reviews methods and interventions that have been demonstrated to be effective in school settings with teen parents. We concentrate on interventions that target decision-making and behavioral skills to help young parents elude many of the associated risks identified earlier, graduate from high school, and ultimately become self-sufficient adults.

# What We Know

### Predictors of Life Outcomes for Adolescent Parents

According to Harris and Franklin (2002), adolescent parents face challenges in four domains that predict their immediate and long-term life outcomes: (1) education, (2) employment, (3) personal relationships, and (4) parenting. Studies show a high degree of interaction among these four outcomes for determining life quality and well-being. For example, evidence indicates that the more supportive a teen mother's relationships with friends and family, the more likely she is to achieve in school and to develop a career (Rhodes & Woods, 1995; Stramenga, 2003; Zupicich, 2003). In turn, the more education an adolescent parent achieves, the higher her employment income is likely to be as an adult (Sandfort & Hill, 1996). Although studies demonstrate the importance of each domain, *education* is the most immediate and well-researched predictor of long-term adjustment and economic status.

### School Achievement

High school graduation or achieving a General Educational Development (GED) before the age of 20 may be the single strongest asset any youth can have to protect against poverty and other negative outcomes in later life (Fine, 1986; Sandfort & Hill, 1996). Thus, school dropout for teen parents may contribute to their at-risk status more than any other factor. Regular attendance and a reasonably age-appropriate grade level, which are major school-related issues for teen parents, are recognized as the most important predictors of whether a student will graduate from high school (Beck, 1991; Burdell, 1998; DeBolt, Pasley, & Kreutzer, 1990). Numerous studies (e.g., Osofsky, Osofsky, & Diamond, 1988; Olah, 1995) indicate that programs focusing on decision-making and behavioral skills that lead to improvement in attendance and grades, personal relationships, and general social competence are the most protective interventions that schools can offer for adolescents who become pregnant. Interventions related to school achievement and dropout prevention and recovery are supported by a sizable group of outcome studies (e.g., Larrivee & Bourque, 1991; Pearson & Banerji, 1993; Rodriguez, 1995; Vallarand, Fortier, & Guay, 1997), although these do not specifically address adolescent parents.

## Alternative Schools of Choice

Programs and services for pregnant and parenting students (as well as other at-risk groups) in many urban school districts are located primarily in alternative schools. These programs are structured academically and provide such additional special courses as sex education, health, life planning, parenting, and job training (Franklin, 1992; Griffin, 1998; Zellman, 1981). Although alternative schools use a variety of models, one that appears to be effective for dropout prevention and retrieval with teen parents and other at-risk populations is a small *school of choice* (Franklin, 1992). The school of choice model offers flexible schedules and individualized, self-paced learning, both compatible with the needs of adolescent parents. In addition, the school of choice model provides student support and advocacy for dealing with psychological, social, and educational barriers to learning and achievement. Although effective interventions specifically for adolescent parents may be more easily established and integrated in an alternative school setting than in a traditional middle or high school, interventions with this population are now demonstrated to be effective in both traditional and alternative school settings (e.g., Fischer, 1997; Griffin, 1998; Harris & Franklin, 2002).

# What We Can Do

## A Cognitive-Behavioral Approach

Skills-building interventions with a cognitive-behavioral foundation are gaining strong support in schools for helping adolescents with a number of problems. Curricula that engage youth in processing logical consequences of behavior and developing mastery of general and specific life skills have been reported to be effective with adolescent issues such as school dropout, pregnancy prevention, adolescent parenting, drug and alcohol addiction, problem school behavior, childhood sexual abuse, and depression (e.g., Barth, 1989; Clarke, 1992; Coren, Barlow, & Stewart-Brown, 2003; Dupper, 1998; Franklin & Corcoran, 1999; Harris & Franklin, 2002; Hogue & Liddle, 1999; McWhirter & Page, 1999). Growing evidence that this approach is effective in a number of areas with pregnant and parenting adolescents (e.g., Codega et al., 1990; Harris & Franklin, 2002) endorses the use of such skills-building intervention in school programs.

## Conditions and Goals of Skills-Based Programs

Skills-based interventions with a cognitive-behavior foundation contain a set of four conditions found to be effective in the mastery of new skills (Hogue & Liddle, 1999):

1. The practitioner models the skill in session.
2. The adolescent role-plays and practices the skill in session.

3. The adolescent is assigned homework to continue practicing the skill.
4. The practitioner debriefs the adolescents about their success in practicing the skill and adjusts skills training to accommodate learning differences.

These interventions appear to be most effective with adolescents when they promote a sense of social support, competence, and self-efficacy. Enhancing internal *locus of control*—the youth's sense that he, rather than forces outside himself, determines the conditions of his life—is often a goal, as well (e.g., McWhirter & Page, 1999; Rice & Meyer, 1994). Specific, *task-related* homework assignments that give the adolescent a chance to practice identified skills, as well as *peer support and feedback*, appear to be effective in reinforcing these personal assets.

A cognitive-behavioral approach seeks to strengthen individual skills such as *coping with stress, problem solving*, and *goal setting* (e.g., Dupper, 1998; Rice & Meyer, 1994). Some interventions target skills specifically related to school achievement, personal relationships, health, and employment (e.g., Griffin, 1998; Harris & Franklin, 2002; Jemmont, Jemmont, Fong, & McCaffree, 1999), which are recognized protectors against the risks associated with teen pregnancy.

## Coping Skills

Adolescents cope with stress in a variety of ways: (1) active, problem-focused strategies, (2) emotional adjustment and acceptance, and (3) avoidance and other passive responses (Olah, 1995; Stern & Alvarez, 1992; Stern & Zevon, 1990). Zeidner and Hammer's (1990) study with teens suggests that the type of coping they use may be more important to resolving stressful situations than the severity or frequency of the stressor. Active, problem-focused coping, found to be more effective in achieving positive outcomes than emotion-focused coping and avoidance (Aspinwall & Taylor, 1992; Zeidner & Hammer, 1990), is often a skill targeted on at-risk adolescents (e.g., Harris & Franklin, 2002). For example, young parents with a tendency to use active, problem-solving coping behaviors are shown repeatedly to experience less stress and to show greater acceptance, warmth, and helpfulness and less disapproval with their children (Colletta & Gregg, 1981; Passino et al., 1993). Even so, studies comparing pregnant to nonpregnant teens show that pregnant teens generally use less active coping than nonpregnant teens, and they identify avoidance or emotion-focused coping as their most frequent strategies (Passino et al., 1993; Codega, Pasley, & Kreutzer, 1990). Thus, increasing problem-focused coping is an important goal for a skills-based intervention with teen parents.

## Social Problem-Solving Skills

Social problem-solving skills are defined as a set of specific attitudes, behaviors, and skills directed toward solving a particular real-life problem in a social context (D'Zurilla, 1986). They include these tasks:

1. Defining and formulating the problem
2. Generating a list of possible solutions

3. Selecting the solution with the best chance to succeed
4. Carrying out the solution strategies
5. Evaluating the outcome

Social problem-solving skills are recognized to strengthen a person's sense of self-efficacy and mastery over one's environment (Bandura, 1999). Although these assets are vital for pregnant and parenting adolescents, research suggests that these youths are less skilled in problem-solving than their nonpregnant peers (Passino et al., 1993). We conclude that problem-solving skills are a vital target for intervention with teen parents.

## Task-Centered Group Modality

With few exceptions, effective skills-based interventions with adolescents are conducted in a group (Glodich & Allen, 1998; e.g., de Anda & Becerra, 1984; Harris & Franklin, 2002; Dupper, 1998). The isolation and need for peer contact and support that often accompany adolescent pregnancy make a group context especially relevant for these youth. Participant focus groups in our outcome studies with young mothers have consistently emphasized that being in a group with other pregnant and parenting students was one of the most important aspects of the intervention (see Box 9.1) (Harris & Franklin, 2004).

We recommend a *task-centered group model* for skills-based intervention with teen parents. This is a form of short-term, goal-oriented treatment in which the client carries out actions or tasks between sessions to alleviate their problems (Reid, 1996). A task-centered group is relatively structured and provides a ready format for skills-based interventions. Over 30 studies have evaluated the effectiveness of task-centered modality, including studies of children with academic problems and adolescents in academic and residential treatment settings (Reid, 1996).

Six to eight members is thought to be the ideal size for a task-centered group, although there is evidence that groups with up to 12 members can also be effective (e.g., Harris & Franklin, 2002). Characteristics such as participants' ages and literacy skills should be considered in determining group size. Two group leaders are considered ideal with this model, although a group can be led by one facilitator when necessary.

# Tools and Practice Examples

## Taking Charge: A Skills-Building Group for Pregnant and Parenting Adolescents

Taking Charge is a task-centered group curriculum for adolescent parents that incorporates the skills-building components and goals discussed in this chapter. Outcome studies in alternative and traditional high schools (Harris & Franklin,

**Box 9.1.** Ways That Task-Centered Groups Fit
the Needs of Adolescent Parents

- *Targets client's abilities.* More than some therapeutic models, task-centered intervention stresses the adolescent's abilities to identify goals and carry through with actions to obtain what she wants. The adolescent parent is assumed to have a mind and a will that are not bound by her age, past experiences, or environment.
- *Focuses on the present.* Task-centered intervention does not attempt to deal with historical origins of the client's problem but rather supports her in achieving its resolution.
- *Short-term.* Most task-centered groups are presented in 6–12 weeks. Short-term interventions are more likely than longer ones to meet program goals within the limited window of access to young parents.
- *Similarity of group members on target problems.* Task-centered groups are best processed when all group members are familiar with the kind of problems others are experiencing and can engage in and benefit from one another's process.

2002; Harris & Franklin, 2004, in review) have demonstrated the Taking Charge curriculum to be effective in achieving these benefits with pregnant and parenting adolescent mothers:

1. School attendance and grades significantly improved.
2. Problem-solving skills significantly improved.
3. Active, problem-focused coping increased significantly.

## Using the Social Problem-Solving Process in Four Life Domains

The Taking Charge program is presented in eight sessions, during which participants learn and apply the social problem-solving process (D'Zurilla & Nezu, 1982) to four important areas of their lives: school achievement, personal relationships, parenting, and career. After learning and practicing the steps, participants use this process during the next sessions to identify and set goals for resolving or mastering problems in each of these areas of their own lives.

These are the steps of the social problem-solving process:

1. Identify a problem that is a real barrier to me in this part of my life.
2. Identify the smaller problems that support this big problem.
3. Describe my goal for resolving this problem.
4. Identify barriers that may happen to keep me from reaching my goal.
5. Name the resources I have that can help me reach my goal.
6. List as many possible strategies as I can to help me reach my goal.
7. Pick a strategy from these that I believe has the best chance to succeed.
8. Decide on two tasks I can do immediately to carry out my strategy.
9. Now…JUST DO IT!

## Brenda: An Example of the Problem-Solving Process

Brenda, aged 16, was a high school junior and the mother of a 3-month-old son. She lived with her 19-year-old boyfriend and his parents. She had lived with the family for 5 months, since before the birth of her baby. Brenda's problem-solving process is set out in Box 9.2.

### Tasks Provide Practice for New Behavior

For each goal they set, group members identify two tasks that are achievable in the week between group sessions. They work with a *"this is my task"* form that guides them through identifying the task and planning how they will carry it out. Some examples of tasks that commonly appear in Taking Charge groups are as follows:

- Meet with my guidance counselor about my (credits, schedule, career plan, etc.).
- Talk to my (math, science, etc.) teacher about my (grade, exam, attitude, etc.).
- Talk to my boyfriend about (help with baby costs, more time together, etc.).
- Spend at least (1 hour, etc.) on homework every day this week.
- Make an appointment to (take baby for shots, apply for food stamps, etc.).

Leaders guide participants in identifying tasks by asking questions and referring to the participants' goal and strategies. They may also help participants rehearse or role-play the task in session.

### Incentives Reinforce New Behavior

To ensure that members receive the greatest benefit from Taking Charge, incentives are built into the group. For example, since food is an important incentive for adolescents and Taking Charge groups often meet during the lunch period, serving lunch during group meetings is one incentive. A snack is served in groups that meet at other times. The lunch or snack is ready to eat immediately when participants arrive.

## Box 9.2. My Personal Relationship Goal

1. MY PROBLEM: My mother-in-law and I don't get along. She's cold to me and criticizes the way I look and dress, how I cook, and especially the way I take care of my baby.

2. SMALLER PROBLEMS: My boyfriend won't stand up to her. I think he's afraid of her. Neither does my father-in-law, even though I get along fine with him. She takes care of my baby while I'm at school, so she's with him as much as I am. My boyfriend is in welding school and only makes minimum wage 20 hours a week at his job, so we're (financially) dependent on his parents for another year. I don't have a car, so she has to take me to appointments for the baby.

3. MY GOAL: For my mother-in-law to like me better and stop criticizing me so much.

4. POSSIBLE BARRIERS: If I try to change anything between us, it may make things worse. I'm scared of her and try to stay away from her. I don't know how to talk to her. I don't like her at all.

5. MY RESOURCES: My boyfriend loves me and wants me to stay. Another resource is my cousin, who's a probation officer. She tries to help me understand my mother-in-law better. Another is my boyfriend's sister, who is cool with me when she drops by, and tells me to ignore my mother-in-law.

6. POSSIBLE STRATEGIES: (1) Confront my mother-in-law and threaten to move out if she doesn't change. (2) Go out of my way to please her without talking about it. (3) Get to know her better. (4) Clear the air with her to find out what I can do to make things better between us. (5) Take my baby and move back to my mother's house.

7. I CHOOSE: The strategy of clearing the air with my mother-in-law and finding out how I can make things better between us.

8. MY FIRST TASK: To talk to my boyfriend's sister about my goal and get her advice on how to talk to her mother. MY SECOND TASK: To tell my mother-in-law that I want to have a good relationship with her and ask her what I can do to help that happen.

A points system is an incentive that allows group members to earn an award at the end of Taking Charge. Points are given for group and school attendance, homework, extra credit assignments, and tasks. Awards are items of particular value to participants, such as gift certificates from a favorite store. Leaders inform the group about the points system at the first session and document points each week.

At two of the eight group sessions participants receive small gifts such as personal grooming items or pizza coupons as they are about to leave the session. In order to maintain this as an incentive for group attendance, the gift is given only to those who attend the sessions at which the gifts are presented.

## Implementing Taking Charge

Even though school-based clinical trials tell us that the Taking Charge curriculum is an effective intervention with adolescent mothers, the ultimate question for school professionals is how easily such a curriculum might be implemented in their school. Anyone working in a school setting knows that there are many things to consider when selecting and implementing social service and mental health programs—How will it impact budget and staff resources? Is it controversial? Is it compatible with the school's educational goals? Will the school staff support it?

Here are some important aspects of this group curriculum to consider when deciding on interventions with pregnant and parenting students.

- In the largest clinical study of the group, the group of young women who participated in the Taking Charge curriculum gained an *eight-point advantage in their GPA* during the semester over an equivalent group who did not participate in the group. The Taking Charge participant group also *increased in school attendance from 79% to 91%*, while the nonparticipants made no gains in attendance.

- A curriculum treatment manual makes it feasible for Taking Charge to be facilitated by volunteers or student interns. The curriculum is compatible with the professional training of school mental health staff, who need only minimal training to supervise volunteer leaders or to facilitate the group.

- The average cost to present the Taking Charge group is $15 to $20 per participant for incentives, in addition to minimal supplies such as paper and folders. In previous Taking Charge studies, lunch or snacks were provided by the school and occasionally donated by local restaurants and businesses.

- In some schools, awards were created using the resources of the school or community that did not involve an outlay of cash. At one school, participants who earned the highest award, and their babies, were treated to a field trip to the city zoo, with school bus transportation and picnic lunches provided by the school cafeteria. At another school, leaders arranged for award recipients to receive manicures and hair styles at a school of cosmetology. In both instances, the alternative award was received enthusiastically by group participants.

- Although the Taking Charge curriculum is not gender-specific for adolescent parents, it has only been studied with young mothers. We cannot assume that it would be as effective with young fathers as with young mothers, although similar developmental needs and societal expectations for young mothers and young fathers suggest that the curriculum may be effective for skills building with young fathers.

- To gain sufficient mastery of the Taking Charge curriculum, we recommend that leaders spend a few hours reviewing and discussing the treatment manual, perhaps with an experienced practitioner or supervisor. Leaders report that they needed to work through the problem-solving process several times with real problems of their own before they felt prepared to help group participants with that process. The extent of training should be determined by the previous training and experience of the leaders.

## Key Points to Remember

Pregnant and parenting adolescents continue to be an at-risk population in schools. With a 60% dropout rate, they are far less likely than their peers to graduate from high school, and they and their children are more likely to live in poverty than parents who delay pregnancy beyond adolescence.

Skills-based interventions that include problem-solving and coping skills have been found to be effective in school programs with other adolescent problems, such as drugs and alcohol, school dropout, and antisocial behavior. Such interventions are gaining support as being effective with teen parents. In this chapter we have examined the foundations of a cognitive-behavioral skills-based approach, as well as the compatibility of using a task-centered group for skills-building interventions. We explored the Taking Charge curriculum, a group intervention for helping adolescent mothers achieve coping and problem-solving skills toward graduating from high school and becoming more competent parents and self-sufficient adults.

# References

## Chapter I

Baker, M. L., Sigmon, J. N., & Nugent, M. E. (2001). *Truancy reduction: Keeping students in school.* Washington, DC: U.S. Department of Justice, Office of Justice Programs, Office of Juvenile Justice and Delinquency Prevention.

Bell, A. J., Rosen, L. A., & Dynlacht, D. (1994). Truancy intervention. *Journal of Research and Development in Education, 57*(3), 203–211.

Borland, M. V., & Howsen, R. M. (1998). Effect of student attendance on performance: Comment on Lamdin. *Journal of Educational Research, 91*(4), 195–197.

Bowen, N. K. (1999). A role for school social workers in promoting student success through school–family partnerships. *Social Work in Education, 21*(1), 34–47.

Catalano, F. R., Arthur, M. W., Hawkins, J. D., Berglund, L., & Olson, J. J. (1998). Comprehensive community- and school-based interventions to prevent antisocial behavior. In R. Loeber & D. Farrington (Eds.), *Serious and violent juvenile offenders: Risk factors and successful interventions* (pp. 248–283). Thousand Oaks, CA: Sage.

Colorado Foundation for Families and Children (2004). Ten things a school can do to improve attendance. Retrieved on October 9, 2004, from http://www.truancyprevention.org/pdf/10_ImproveAttendance.pdf

Corville-Smith, J., Ryan, B. A., Adams, G. R., & Dalicandro, T. (1998). Distinguishing absentee students from regular attenders: The combined influence of personal, family, and school factors. *Journal of Youth and Adolescence, 27*(5), 629–637.

Dryfoos, J. G. (1990). *Adolescents at risk: Prevalence and prevention.* New York: Oxford University Press.

Dynarski, M., & Gleason, P. (1999). *How can we help? Lessons from federal dropout prevention programs.* Princeton, NJ: Mathematica Policy Research.

Epstein, J. L., & Sheldon, S. B. (2002). Present and accounted for: Improving student attendance through family and community involvement. *Journal of Educational Research, 95*(5), 308–318.

Fallis, R. K., & Opotow, S. (2003). Are students failing school or are schools failing students? Class cutting in high school. *Journal of Social Issues, 59*(1), 103–119.

Finn, J. D., & Voelkl, K. E. (1993). School characteristics related to school engagement. *Journal of Negro Education, 62*, 249–268.

Ford, J., & Sutphen, R. D. (1996). Early intervention to improve attendance in elementary school at-risk children: A pilot program. *Social Work in Education, 18*(2), 95–102.

Huizinga, D., Loeber, R., & Thornberry, T. (1995). *Urban delinquency and substance abuse: Initial findings.* Washington, DC: U.S. Department of Justice, Office of Justice Programs, Office of Juvenile Justice and Delinquency Prevention.

Kearney, C.A. (2003). Bridging the gap among professionals who address youths with school absenteeism: Overview and suggestions for consensus. *Professional Psychology: Research and Practice, 34*(1), 57–65.

Lamdin, D. J. (2001). Evidence of student attendance as an independent variable in education production functions. *Journal of Educational Research, 89*(3), 155–162.

Loeber, R., & Farrington, D. (2000). Young children who commit crime: Epidemiology, developmental origins, risk factors, early interventions, and policy implications. *Development and Psychopathology, 12*(4), 737–762.

Miller, D. (2002). Effect of a program of therapeutic discipline on the attitude, attendance, and insight of truant adolescents. *Journal of Experimental Education, 55*(1), 49–53.

Reid, W. J., & Bailey-Dempsey, C. (1995). The effects of monetary incentives on school performance. *Families in Society, 76*(6), 331–340.

Robins, L. N., & Ratcliff, K. S. (1978). *Long-range outcomes associated with school truancy.* Washington, DC: Public Health Service.

Rohrman, D. (1993). Combating truancy in our schools—a community effort. *NASSP (National Association of Secondary School Principals) Bulletin, 76*(77), 40–45.

Snyder, H. N., & Sickmund, M. (1995). *Juvenile offenders and victims: A national report.* Washington, DC: U.S. Department of Justice, Office of Justice Programs, Office of Juvenile Justice and Delinquency Prevention.

Sturgeon, R., & Beer, J. (1990). Attendance reward and absenteeism in high school.

# Chapter 2

Adelman, H., & Taylor, L. (2003). *Addressing barriers to learning: A comprehensive approach to mental health in schools.* Los Angeles, LA: Center for Mental Health in Schools at UCLA.

Bowen, G. L., Woolley, M., Richman, J. M., & Bowen, N. K. (2001). Brief intervention in schools: The school success profile. *Brief Treatment and Crisis Intervention, 1*, 43–54.

Bowen, N. K., & Bowen, G. L. (1999). Effects of crime and violence in neighborhoods and schools on the school behavior and performance of adolescents. *Journal of Adolescent Research, 14*, 319–342.

Bowen, N. K., & Bowen, G. L. (2001). *The school success profile.* Chapel Hill, NC: University of North Carolina Press.

Cartledge G., & Milburn, J. F. (1996). *Cultural diversity and social skills instruction.* Champaign, IL: Research Press.

Deschenes, S., Cuban, L., & Tyack, D. (2001). Mismatch: Historical perspectives on schools and students who don't fit. *Teachers College Record, 103*, 525–547.

Dimmitt, C. (2003). Transforming school counseling practice through collaboration and the use of data: A study of academic failure in high school. *Professional School Counseling, 6*(5), 340–349.

Durlak, J. A. (1995). *School-based prevention programmes for children and adolescents.* Thousand Oaks, CA: Sage.

Dwyer, K., & Osher, D. (2000). *Safeguarding our children: An action guide.* Washington, DC: U.S. Department of Education and Justice, American Institutes of Research.

Friedberg, R. D., & McClure, J. M. (2002). *Clinical practice of cognitive therapy with children and adolescents: The nuts and bolts.* New York: Guilford.

Hawkins, J. D., Arthur, M. W., & Catalano, R. F. (1995). Preventing substance abuse. In M. Tonry & D. Farrington (Eds.), *Crime and justice: A review of research. Building a safer society: Strategic approaches to crime prevention* (Vol. 19, pp. 343–427). Chicago, IL: University of Chicago Press.

Hoagwood, K., & Johnson, J. (2003). School psychology: A public health framework; I. From evidence-based practices to evidence-based policies. *Journal of School Psychology, 41*, 3–21.

Huffman, L., Mehlinger, S., & Kerivan, A. (2000). *Research on the risk factors for early school problems and selected federal policies affecting children's social and emotional development and their readiness for school.* Child Mental Health Foundation and Agencies Network. Retrieved May 16, 2004, from www.nimh.nih.gov/childp/goodstart.cfm

Kao, G., & Thompson, J. S. (2003). Racial and ethnic stratification in educational achievement and attainment. *Annual Review of Sociology, 29*, 417–442.

Kaufman, P., Kwon, J. Y., Klein, S., & Chapman, C. (2000). *Dropout rates in the United States* (NCES 2001–2002). Washington, DC: U.S. Department of Education National Center for Education Statistics.

Kazdin, A. E. (2003). Problem-solving skills training and parent management training for conduct disorder. In A. Kazdin & J. R. Weisz (Eds.), *Evidence-based psychotherapies for children and adolescents.* New York: Guilford.

Knoff, H. M. (2001). *The stop and think social skills program (preschool–grade 1, grades 2/3, grades 4/5, middle school 6–8).* Longmont, CO: Sopris West.

Knoff, H. M., Finch, C., & Carlyon, W. (2004). Project ACHIEVE and the development of school-wide positive behavioral self-management systems—prevention, intervention, and intensive needs approaches. In K. E. Robinson, *Advances in school-based mental health interventions: Best practices and program models* (pp. 19-1–19-28). Kingston, NJ: Civic Research Institute.

Lonigan, C. J., Elbert, J. C., & Johnson, S. B. (1998). Empirically supported psychosocial interventions for children: An overview. *Journal of Child Clinical Psychology, 27*, 138–145.

McFarland, W. P., & Dupois, M. (2001). The legal duty to protect gay and lesbian students from violence in the schools. *Professional School Counseling, 4*(3), 171–180.

Nash, J. K. (2002). Neighborhood effects on sense of school coherence and educational behavior in students at risk of school failure. *Children and Schools, 24*, 73–89.

O'Keefe, M. (1994). Adjustment of children from maritally violent homes. *Families in Society, 75*, 403–415.

Owings, W. A., & Magliaro, S. (1998). Grade retention: A history of failure. *Educational Leadership, 56*(1), 86–89.

Raffaele, L., & Knoff, H. (1999). Improving home-school collaboration with disadvantaged families: Organizational principles, perspectives, and approaches. *School Psychology Review, 28*, 448–466.

Richman, J. M., Bowen, G. L., & Woolley, M. E. (2004). School failure: An eco-interactional developmental perspective. In M. W. Fraser (Ed.), *Risk and resilience in childhood: An ecological perspective* (2nd ed., pp. 133–160). Washington, DC: NASW Press.

Scheurich, J. J., Skrla, L., & Johnson, J. F. (2000). Thinking carefully about equity and accountability. *Phi Delta Kappan, 82*(4), 293–300.

Sheridan, S. M., Eagle, J. W., Cowan, R. J., & Mickelson, W. (2001). The effects of conjoint behavioral consultation: Results of a four-year investigation. *Journal of School Psychology, 39*, 361–385.

Sheridan, S. M., & Kratochwill, T. R. (1992). Behavioral parent–teacher consultation: Conceptual and research considerations. *Journal of School Psychology, 30*, 117–139.

Stallard, P. (2002). *Think good—feel good: A cognitive behavior therapy workbook for children and young people.* Hoboken, NJ: John Wiley & Sons.

Weisz, J. R., & Jensen, P. S. (1999). Efficacy and effectiveness of child and adolescent psychotherapy and pharmacotherapy. *Mental Health Services Research, 1*, 125–157.

# Chapter 3

Amenta, R. (1997). Horizon alternative school: Why promising reforms disappear. *Education Week, 16*(22), 36, 38.

Ascher, C. (1982). ERIC/CUE: Alternative schools: Some answers and questions. *Urban Review, 14*, 65–69.

Atkins, T., Allen, J., & Meredith, M. (n.d.). *Alternative schools: Information for families.* Eugene: Center for Effective Collaboration and Practice, University of Oregon. Retrieved April 6, 2004, from http:// cecp.air.org/familybriefs/docs/AltSch.pdf

Barr, R. D., & Parrett, W. H. (2001). *Hope fulfilled for at-risk and violent youth.* Needham Heights, MA: Allyn & Bacon.

Chavkin, N. F. (1993). School social workers helping multiethnic families: Schools and communities join forces. In N. F. Chavkin (Ed.), *Families and schools in a pluralistic society* (pp. 217–228). Albany, NY: State University of New York Press.

Cox, S. M., Davidson, W. S., & Bynum, T. S. (1995). A meta-analytic assessment of delinquency-related outcomes of alternative education programs. *Crime and Delinquency, 41*, 219–234.

DeBlois, R. (1994). Keeping alternatives alive. *American School Board Journal, 181*, 33–34.

Dollar, R. (1983). What is really going on in schools? *Social Policy, 13*, 7–19.

Dugger, C., & DesMoulin-Kherat, S. (1996). Helping younger dropouts get back into school. *Middle School Journal, 28*, 29–33.

Dupper, D. R. (1993). School-community collaboration: A description of a model program designed to prevent school dropouts. *School Social Work Journal, 18*, 32–39.

*Education World.* (1998). Where everyone knows your name! Special programs target at-risk students. Retrieved April 20, 2004, from http://www.educationworld.com/a_admin/admin098.shtml

Franklin, C., & Streeter, C. L. (1991). Evidence for the effectiveness of social work with high school dropout youths. *Social Work in Education, 13*, 307–327.

Glass, R. (1995). Alternative schools help kids succeed. *Education Digest, 60*, 21–24.

Gregg, S. (1998). *Schools for disruptive students: A questionable alternative?* Policy Briefs series. Charleston, WV: Appalachia Educational Laboratory.

Harrington-Lueker, D. (1994). Hanging on to hope. *American School Board Journal, 181,* 16–21.

Ingersoll, S., & LeBoeuf, D. (1997). *Reaching out to youth out of the education mainstream.* U.S. Department of Justice, Office of Justice Programs, Office of Juvenile Justice and Delinquency Prevention.

Kadel, S. (1994). *Reengineering high schools for student access. Hot topics: Usable research.* Palatha, FL: Southeastern Regional Vision for Education (ERIC Document Reproduction Service No. ED366076).

Kellmayer, J. (1995). *How to establish an alternative school.* Thousand Oaks, CA: Corwin.

Kershaw, C., & Blank, M. (1993, April). *Student and educator perceptions of the impact of an alternative school structure.* Paper presented at the annual meeting of the American Educational Research Association, Atlanta, GA.

Kraemer, J., & Ruzzi, B. B. (2001). Alternative education cannot be left behind. *Education Week.* Retrieved January 23, 2004, from http://www.edweek.org/ew/newstory.cfm?slug=06kraemer.h21

Lange, C. M., & Sletten, S. J. (2002). *Alternative education: A brief history and research synthesis.* Alexandria, VA: National Association of State Directors of Special Education.

McGee, J. (2001). Reflections of an alternative school administrator. *Phi Delta Kappan, 82,* 588–591.

Morley, R. (1991). *Alternative education* (ED349652). Clemson, SC: National Dropout Prevention Center.

National Conference of State Legislatures. (2004). Successful alternative education programs for troubled youth. Retrieved May 1, 2004, from http://ncsl.org/programs/educ/AlterEdSN.htm

North Carolina Education and Law Project. (1997). *Alternative schools: Short-term solutions with long-term consequences* (2nd ed.). Raleigh, NC: Author.

Northwest Regional Educational Laboratory. (2001). *Alternative schools: Approaches for students at risk.* Retrieved May 1, 2004, from http://www.nwrel.org/request/sept97/article2.html

Public Schools of North Carolina. (2000, March). Case studies of best practices. Alternative schools and programs: 1998–99. Raleigh, NC: Author. Retrieved May 5, 2004, from http://www.ncpublicschool.org/accountability/alternative/case9899.pdf

Raywid, M. (1990). Alternative education: The definition problem. *Changing Schools, 18,* 4–5, 10.

Raywid, M. (1994). Synthesis of research: Alternative schools: The state of the art. *Educational Leadership, 52,* 26–31.

Reimer, M. S., & Cash, T. (2003). *Alternative schools: Best practices for development and evaluation.* Clemson, SC: National Dropout Prevention Center/Network.

Schargel, F. P., & Smink, J. (2001). *Strategies to help solve our school dropout problem.* Larchmont, NY: Eye on Education.

U.S. Department of Education (1996). *Safe and drug-free schools. Alternative education programs for expelled students.* Retrieved May 1, 2004, from http://www.ed.gov/offices/OESE/SDFS/actguid/altersc.html

U.S. Department of Education. (2002). *Characteristics of the 100 largest elementary and secondary school districts in the United States: 2000–01*, NCES 2002–351. Washington DC: Author.

Wehlage, G. (1983). *Effective programs for the marginal high school student. Fastback 197*. Bloomington, IN: Phi Delta Kappa.

Young, T. (1990). *Public alternative education: Options and choices for today's schools.* New York: Teachers College Press.

# Chapter 4

Aloise-Young, P. A., & Chavez, E. L. (2002). Not all school dropouts are the same: Ethnic differences in the relation between reason for leaving school and adolescent substance use. *Psychology in the Schools, 39*(5), 539–547.

Berg, I. K., & De Jong, P. (1996). Solution-building conversation: Co-constructing a sense of competence with clients. *Families in Society: The Journal of Contemporary Human Services, 77*, 376–391.

Berg, I. K., & Shilts, L. (2005). *Classroom solutions: WOWW approach*. Milwaukee, WI: Brief Family Therapy Center.

Corcoran, J. (1998). Solution-focused practice with middle and high school at-risk youths. *Social Work in Education, 20*(4), 232–244.

Corcoran, J., & Stephenson, M. (2000). The effectiveness of solution-focused therapy with child behavior problems: A preliminary study. *Families in Society, 81*(5), 468–474.

De Jong, P., & Berg, I. K. (2001). Co-constructing cooperation with mandated clients. *Social Work, 46*(4), 361–381.

De Jong, P., & Berg, I. K. (2002). *Interviewing for solutions* (2nd ed.). Pacific Grove, CA: Brooks/Cole.

de Shazer, S. (1985). *Keys to solution in brief therapy.* New York: Norton.

Franklin, C., Biever, J., Moore, K., Clemons, D., & Scamardo, M. (2001). The effectiveness of solution-focused therapy with children in a school setting. *Research on Social Work Practice, 11*(4), 411–434.

Franklin, C., Corcoran, J., Nowicki, J., & Streeter, C. (1997). Using client self-anchored scales to measure outcomes in solution-focused therapy. *Journal of Systemic Therapies, 10*(3), 246–265.

Franklin, C., & Moore, K. C. (1999). Solution-focused brief family therapy. In C. Franklin & C. Jordan, *Family practice: Brief systems methods for social work* (pp. 143–174). Pacific Grove, CA: Brooks/Cole.

Franklin, C., & Nurius, P. (1998). Distinction between social constructionism and cognitive constructivism: Practice applications. In C. Franklin & P. Nurius (Eds.), *Constructivism in practice: Methods and challenges* (pp. 57–94). Milwaukee, WI: Families International.

Franklin, C., & Streeter, C. L. (2003). *Solution-focused accountability schools for the 21st century: A training manual for Garza High School.* Austin: University of Texas, Hogg Foundation for Mental Health.

Franklin, C., & Streeter, C. L. (2005). *Solution-focused alternatives for education: An Evaluation of Gonzalo Garza Independent High School.* Austin: University of Texas, Hogg Foundation for Mental Health.

Hawkes, D., Marsh, T., & Wilgosh, R. (1998). How to begin: The concepts of solution-focused therapy. In *Solution focused therapy: A handbook for health care professionals* (pp. 5–15). Woburn, MA: Reed.

Hopson, L. M., & Kim, J. S. (2004). A solution-focused approach to crisis intervention with adolescents. *Journal of Evidence-Based Social Work, 1*(2–3), 93–110.

Jordan, W. L., Lara, J., & McPartland, J. M. (1996). Exploring the causes of early dropout among race-ethnic and gender groups. *Youth & Society, 28*(1), 62–94.

Kral, R. (1995). *Strategies that work: Techniques for solutions in schools.* Milwaukee, WI: Brief Family Therapy Press.

LaFountain, R. M., & Garner, N. E. (1996). Solution-focused counseling groups: The results are in. *Journal for Specialists in Group Work, 21*(2), 128–143.

Lathem, J. (2002). Brief solution-focused therapy. *Child and Adolescent Mental Health, 7*(4), 189–192.

Lee, M. Y. (Ed.). (1997). A study of solution-focused brief family therapy: Outcomes and issues. *American Journal of Family Therapy, 25,* 3–17.

Littrell, J. M., Malia, J. A., & Vanderwood, M. (1995). Single-session brief counseling in a high school. *Journal of Counseling and Development, 73,* 451–458.

Metcalf, L. (1995). *Counseling toward solutions: A practical solution-focused program for working with students, teachers, and parents.* San Francisco, CA: Jossey-Bass.

Miller, G., & de Shazer, S. (2000). Emotions in solution-focused therapy: A re-examination. *Family Process, 39*(1), 5.

Moore, K. C., & Franklin, C. (2005). The effectiveness of solution-focused therapy with school-related behavior problems. Manuscript under review

Murphy, J. (1996). Solution-focused brief therapy in the school. In S. Miller, M. Hubble, & B. Duncan (Eds.), *Handbook of solution-focused brief therapy* (pp. 184–204). San Francisco: Jossey-Bass.

National Dropout Prevention Center. (2004). *National Dropout Prevention Center/ Network: Effective strategies.* Available: http://www.dropoutprevention.org/effstrat/effstrat.htm

Newsome, S. (2004). Solution-focused brief therapy (SFBT) groupwork with at-risk junior high school students: Enhancing the bottom-line. *Research on Social Work Practice, 14*(5), 336–343.

Pichot, T., & Dolan, Y. (2003). *Solution-focused brief therapy: Its effective use in agency settings.* Binghamton, NY: Hawthorne.

Prevatt, F., & Kelly, F. D. (2003). Dropping out of school: A review of intervention programs. *Journal of School Psychology, 5,* 377–395.

Rumberger, R. W. (1987). High school dropouts: A review of issues and evidence. *Review of Educational Research, 57*(2), 101–121.

Rumberger, R. W. (2004). Why students drop out of school. In G. Orfied (Ed.), *Dropouts in America: Confronting the graduation rate crisis* (pp. 131–155). Cambridge, MA: Harvard Education Press.

Rumberger, R. W., Ghatak, R., Poulos, G., Ritter, P. L., & Dornbusch, S. M. (1990). Family influences on dropout behavior in one California high school. *Sociology of Education, 63,* 283–299.

Rumberger, R. W., & Thomas, S. L. (2000). The distribution of dropout and turn-over rates among urban and suburban high school. *Sociology of Education, 73*(1), 39–67.

Sklare, G. (1997). *Brief counseling that works: A solution-focused approach for school counselors* (pp. 43–64). Thousand Oaks, CA: Corwin Press/Sage.

Slavin, R. E., & Fashola, O. S. (1998). *Show me the evidence: Proven and promising programs for America's schools.* New York: Corwin Press.

Springer, D., Lynch, C., & Rubin, A. (2000). Effects of a solution-focused mutual aid group for Hispanic children of incarcerated parents. *Child & Adolescent Social Work Journal, 17*(6), 431–442.

Walter, J. L., & Peller, J. E. (1996). Rethinking our assumptions: Assuming anew in a postmodern world. In S. Miller, M. Hubble, & B. Duncan (Eds.), *Handbook of solution-focused brief therapy* (pp. 9–26). San Francisco: Jossey-Bass.

Webb, W. H. (1999). *Solutioning: Solution-focused interventions for counselors.* Philadelphia: Accelerated Press.

What Works Clearinghouse. (n.d.). *Interventions for preventing high school dropout.* Available: http://www.w-w-c.org/comingnext/dropout.html

## Chapter 5

Bandura, A. (2002). Social cognitive theory in cultural context. *Applied Psychology, 51*, 269–290.

Brave Heart, M. Y. H. (1998). The return to the sacred path: Healing historical trauma response among the Lakota. *Smith College Studies in Social Work, 68*(3), 287–305.

Brave Heart, M. Y. H. (2001a). Culturally and historically congruent clinical social work assessment with Native clients. In R. Fong & S. Furuto (Eds.), *Cultural competent social work practice: Practice skills* (pp. 163–177). Needham Heights, MA: Allyn & Bacon.

Brave Heart, M. Y. H. (2001b). Culturally and historically congruent interventions with Native clients. In R. Fong & S. Furuto (Eds.), *Cultural competent social work practice: Practice skills* (pp. 285–298). Needham Heights, MA: Allyn & Bacon.

Farkas, G. (2003). Racial disparities and discrimination in education: What do we know, how do we know it, and what do we need to know? *Teachers College Record, 105*(6), 1119–1146.

Franklin, C., & Jordan, C. (2003). An integrative skills assessment approach. In C. Jordan & C. Franklin (Eds.), *Clinical assessment for social workers: Quantitative and qualitative methods* (2nd ed.). Chicago: Lyceum.

Gilbert, D. J. (2003) Multicultural assessment: A focus on ethnic-minority clients. In C. Jordan, & C. Franklin, *Clinical assessment for social workers: Quantitative and qualitative methods* (2nd ed., pp. 351–383). Chicago: Lyceum.

Gilbert, D. J., & Franklin, C. (2001). Evaluation skills with Native American individuals and families, In R. Fong & S. Furuto (Eds.), *Cultural competent social work practice: Practice skills* (pp. 178–195). Needham Heights, MA: Allyn & Bacon.

LaFromboise, T., & Dixon, M. R. (2003). American Indian children and adolescents. In J. Taylor Gibbs, L. N. Huang, & associates (Eds.), *Children of color: Psychological interventions with culturally diverse youth.* San Francisco, CA: Jossey-Bass.

LaFromboise, T., & Howard-Pitney, B. (1995). The Zuni Life Skills Development Curriculum: Description and evaluation of a suicide prevention program. *Journal of Counseling Psychology, 42*, 479–486.

Ogunwole, S. (2002). *The American Indian and Alaska Native population: 2000.* Washington, DC: U.S. Bureau of the Census, U.S. Department of Commerce.

Pavel, D. M. (1995). Comparing BIA and tribal schools with public schools. *Journal of American Indian Education, 35*(1).

Sanchez-Way, R., & Johnson, C. (2000). Cultural practices in American Indian prevention programs. *Juvenile Justice, 7*(92), 20–30.

Weaver, H. (2001). Organization and community assessment with First Nations people. In R. Fong & S. Furuto (Eds.), *Cultural competent social work practice: Practice skills* (pp. 178–195). Needham Heights, MA: Allyn & Bacon.

Yellow Bird, M. (2001). Critical values and First Nations peoples. In R. Fong & S. Furuto (Eds.), *Cultural competent social work practice: Practice skills* (pp. 61–74). Needham Heights, MA: Allyn & Bacon.

Yellow Horse, S., & Brave Heart, M. Y. H. (2004 ). A review of the literature. Healing the Wakanheja: Evidence based, promising, and culturally appropriate practices for American Indian/Alaska Native children with mental health needs. In A. D. Strode (Ed.), *Mental health best practices for vulnerable populations* (pp. 35–43). Washington State Department of Social and Health Services, Mental Health Division.

# Chapter 6

Astor, R. A., Behre, W. J., Wallace, J. M., & Fravil, K. (1998). School social workers and school violence: Personal safety, training, and violence programs. *Social Work, 43*(3), 223–232.

Catalano, R. F., Berglund, M. L., Ryan, J. A. M., Lonczak, H. S., & Hawkins, J. D. (2002). Positive youth development in the United States: Research findings on evaluations of positive youth development programs. *Prevention & Treatment, 5*, Article 15. Available: http://journals.apa.org/prevention

Daro, D. A., & Harding, K. A. (1999). Healthy Families America: Using research to enhance practice. *Future of Children, 9*(1), 152–176.

Duggan, A., Fuddy, L., Burrell, L., Higman, S. M., McFarlane, E., Windham, A., & Sia, C. (2004). Randomized trail of a statewide home visiting program to prevent child abuse: Impact in reducing parental risk factors. *Child Abuse and Neglect, 28*, 623–643.

Fraser, M. W., Day, S. V., Galinsky, M. J., Hodges, V. G., & Smokowski, P. R. (2004). Conduct problems and peer rejection in childhood: A randomized trial of the Making Choices and Strong Families programs. *Research on Social Work Practice, 14*, 313–324.

Gomby, D. S., Culross, P. L., & Behrman, R. E. (1999). Home visiting: Recent program evaluations: Analysis and recommendations. *Future of Children: Home Visiting, 9*, 4–26.

Gomby, D. S., Larson, C. S., Lewit, E. M., & Behrman, R. E. (1993). Home visiting: Analysis and recommendations. *Future of Children: Home Visiting, 3*, 6–22.

Greenberg, M. T., Domitrovich, C., & Bumbarger, B. (2001). The prevention of mental disorders in school-aged children: Current state of the field. *Prevention & Treatment, 4*, Article 1. Available: http://journals.apa.org/prevention

Guterman, N. B. (2000). *Stopping child maltreatment before it starts: Emerging horizons in early home visitation services.* Thousand Oaks, CA: Sage.

Hancock, B. L., & Pelton, L. H. (1989). Home visits: History and functions. *Social Casework, 70*, 21–27.

Henggeler, S. W., Schoenwald, S. K., Borduin, C. M., Rowland, M. D., & Cunningham, P. B. (1998). *Multisystemic treatment of antisocial behavior in children and adolescents.* New York: Guilford.

Johnson, K. A. (2001). *No place like home: State home visiting policies and programs.* Commonwealth Fund. Available: http://www.cmwf.org/publications/publications_show.htm?doc_id=221347

Levine, M., & Levine, A. (1970). *A social history of the helping services: Clinic, court, school, and community.* New York: Appleton-Century-Crofts.

Lutzker, J. R., Bigelow, K. M., Doctor, R. M., Gershater, R. M., & Greene, B. F. (1998). An ecological behavioral model for the prevention and treatment of child abuse and neglect. In J. R. Lutzker (Ed.), *Handbook of child abuse research and treatment* (pp. 239–266). New York: Plenum.

Minuchin, P., Colapinto, J., & Minuchin, S. (1998). *Working with families of the poor.* New York: Guilford.

Olds, D. L., Henderson, C. R., Kitzman, H. J., Eckenrode, J. J., Cole, R. E., & Tatelbaum, R. C. (1999). Prenatal and infant home visitation by nurses: Recent findings. *Future of Children, 9,* 44–65.

Oppenheimer, J. J. (1925). *The visiting teacher movement with special reference to administrative relationships* (2nd ed.). New York: Joint Committee on Methods of Preventing Delinquency.

Richmond, M. (1899). *Friendly visiting among the poor.* New York: Macmillan.

Substance Abuse and Mental Health Services Administration, Center for Substance Abuse Prevention. (n.d.) *SAMHSA model programs: Effective substance abuse and mental health programs for every community.* Available: http://modelprograms.samhsa.gov

Sweet, M. A., & Appelbaum, M. I. (2004). Is home visiting an effective strategy? A meta-analytic review of home visiting programs for families with young children. *Child Development, 75*(5), 1435–1456.

Wasik, B. H., & Bryant, D. M. (2001). *Home visiting: Procedures for helping families* (2nd ed.). Thousand Oaks, CA: Sage.

Wasik, B. H., & Coleman, S. (2004). *Safety issues in home visiting.* Chapel Hill, NC: Center for Home Visiting, University of North Carolina.

Wasik, B. H., & Sparling, J. J. (1998). *Home Visit Assessment Instrument.* Chapel Hill, NC: Center for Home Visiting, University of North Carolina.

# Chapter 7

Atkins, M. S., Adil, J., Jackson, M., Talbott, E., & Bell, C. (2001). School-based mental health services in urban schools: An ecological approach. *Report on Emotional and Behavioral Disorders in Youth 1*(4), 75–93.

Atkins, M. S., Graczyk, P., Frazier, S., & Adil, J. (2003a). School mental health in urban communities. In M. Weist, S. Evans, & N. Lever (Eds.), *School mental health handbook* (pp. 165–178). New York: Kluwer.

Atkins, M., Graczyk, P., Frazier, S., & Adil, J. (2003b). Toward a new model for school-based mental health: Accessible, effective, and sustainable services in urban communities. *School Psychology Review, 12,* 503–514.

Atkins, M. S., McKay, M. M., Arvantis, P., London, L., Madison, S., Costigan, C., et al. (1998). An ecological model for school-based mental health services for urban low-income aggressive children. *Journal of Behavioral Health Services and Research* 5(1), 64–75.

Axelrod, S. (1977). *Behavior modifications for the classroom teacher.* New York: McGraw-Hill.

Battistich, V., Schaps, E., Watson, M., & Solomon, D. (1996). Prevention effects of the Child Development Project: Early findings from an ongoing multisite demonstration trial. *Journal of Adolescent Research, 11,* 12–35.

Catron, T., & Weiss, B. (1994). The Vanderbilt school–based counseling program: An interagency, primary-care model of mental health services. *Journal of Emotional and Behavioral Disorders, 2,* 247–253.

Clarke, G., Hawkins, W., Murphy, M., Sheeber, L., Lewinsohn, P., & Seeley, J. (1995). Targeted prevention of unipolar depressive disorder in an at-risk sample of high school adolescents: A randomized trial of a group cognitive intervention. *Journal of the American Academy of Child and Adolescent Psychiatry, 34,* 312–321.

Comer, J. P., Haynes, N. M., Joyner, E. T., & Ben-Avie, M. (1996). *Rallying the whole village: The Comer process for reforming education.* New York: Teachers College Press.

Cox, M. E., Orme, J. G., & Rhodes, K. W. (2003). Willingness to foster children with emotional or behavioral problems. *Journal of Social Service Research, 29*(4), 23–51.

Hawkins, J. D., Catalano, R. F., Kosterman, R., Abbott, R., & Hill, K. (1999). Preventing adolescent health-risk behaviors by strengthening protection during childhood. *Archives of Pediatric and Adolescent Medicine, 153,* 226–234.

Mash, E. J., & Barkley, R. A. (Eds.). (1989). *Treatment of childhood disorders.* New York: Guilford.

Mayer, G. R. (1995). Preventing antisocial behavior in school. *Journal of Behavioral Analysis, 28,* 467–478.

Slavin, R., Karweit, N. L., & Wasik, B. (1994). *Preventing early school failure.* Needham Heights, MA: Allyn & Bacon.

Zigler, E. F. (1989). Addressing the nation's child care crisis: The school of the 21st century. *American Journal of Orthopsychiatry, 59,* 485–491.

# Chapter 8

Advocates for Youth. (2003). Science and success: Sex education and other programs that work to prevent teen pregnancy, HIV, and sexually transmitted infections. Washington, DC: Author. Accessed online November 12, 2004, at http://www. advocatesforyouth.org/publications/ScienceSuccess.pdf

Afexentiou, D., & Hawley, C. B. (1997). Explaining female teenagers' sexual behavior and outcomes: A bivariate probit analysis with selectivity correction. *Journal of Family and Economic Issues, 18*(1), 91–106.

Alan Guttmacher Institute. (2004). U.S. teenage pregnancy statistics: Overall trends, trends by race and ethnicity and state-by state information. Retrieved November 12, 2004, from www.guttmacher.org/pus/ state_pregnancy_trends.pdf

Allen, J. P., Philliber, S., Herrling, S., & Kuperminc, G. P. (1997). Preventing teen pregnancy and academic failure: Experimental evaluation of a developmentally-based approach. *Child Development, 64*(4), 729–742.

Card, J. J., Niego, S., Mallari, A., & Farrell, W. S. (1996). Prevention programs in a box. Family Planning Perspectives, 285, 210–220. Retrieved on November 29, 2004, from www.agi-usa.org/pubs/journals/2821096.html

Child Trends. (2001). Retrieved on November 24, 2004, from http://www.childtrends. org/PDF/KnightReports/KRepro.pdf

Child Trends. (2002). Retrieved on November 27, 2004, from http://www.childtrends. org/PDF/KnightReports/KRepro.pdf

Denner, J., Coyle, K., Robin, L., & Banspach, S. (2005). Integrating service learning into a curriculum to reduce health risks at alternative high schools. *Journal of School Health, 75*(5), 151–157.

Franklin, C., & Corcoran, J. (2000). Preventing adolescent pregnancy: A review of programs and practices. *Social Work, 45*(1), 40–52.

Haeman, R. H., Wolfe, B., & Peterson, E. (1997). Children of early childbearers as young adults. In R. A. Maynard (Ed.), *Kids having kids: Economic costs and social consequences of teen pregnancy* (pp. 257–284). Washington, DC: Urban Institute Press.

Jindal, B. P. (2001). Report to House Committee on Ways and Means Subcommittee on Human Resources November 15. Washington, DC: U.S. Government.

Kirby, D. (2001). *Emerging answers: Research findings on programs to reduce teen pregnancy.* Washington, DC: National Campaign to Prevent Teen Pregnancy.

Manlove, J., Franzetta, K., McKinney, K., Papillo, A. R., & Terry-Humen, E. (2004). *A good time: After-school programs to reduce teen pregnancy. National Campaign to Prevent Teen Pregnancy.* Washington, DC: Author.

Manlove, J., Terry-Humen, E., Papillo, A. R., Franzetta, K., Williams, S., & Ryan, S. (2001). *Background for community-level work on positive reproductive health in adolescence: Reviewing the literature on contributing factors.* Washington, DC: Child Trends. Retrieved online November 23, 2004, at www.childtrends.org/ PDF/ KnightReports/KRepro.pdf

Manlove, J., Terry-Humen, E., Papillo, A. R., Franzetta, K., Williams, S., & Ryan, S. (2002). *Preventing teenage pregnancy, childbearing, and sexually transmitted diseases: What the research shows.* Washington, DC: Child Trends. Retrieved November 22, 2004, at www. childtrends.org/PDF/Knightreports/K1Brief.pdf

Melchoir, A. (1998). National evaluation of learn and serve America school and community-based programs: Final report. Abt Associates, Inc., Cambridge, MA; Brandeis University, Waltham, MA. Center for National Service.

National Campaign to Prevent Teen Pregnancy. (2002). *Teen pregnancy: Not just another single issue.* Washington, DC: Author.

National Campaign to Prevent Teen Pregnancy. (2004). *Fact sheet: How is the 34% statistic calculated?* Washington, DC: Author.

PASHA Programs Table. (2002). Accessed online at http://www.socio.com/newpasha/ pashatablebox1. htm

Philliber, S., & Allen, J. P. (1992). Life options and community service: Teen outreach program. In B. C. Miller, J. J. Card, R. L. Paikoff, & J. L. Peterson (Eds.), *Preventing adolescent pregnancy: Model programs and evaluations* (pp. 139–155). Newbury Park, CA: Sage.

Philliber, S., Williams Kaye, J., & Herrling, S. (2001). *The national evaluation of the Children's Aid Society Carrera-model program to prevent teen pregnancy.* Accord, NY: Philliber Research Associates.

Philliber, S., Williams Kaye, J., Herrling, S., & West, E. (2002). Preventing pregnancy and improving health care access among teenagers: An evaluation of the Children's Aid Society—Carrera program. *Perspectives on Sexual and Reproductive Health, 34*(5), 244–252.

Schlitt, J. J., Rickitt, K. D., Montgomery, L. L., & Lear, J. G. (1994). State initiatives to support school-based health centers: A national survey. Paper presented at NASW Annual Conference, Memphis.

Singh, S., & Darroch, J. E. (2000). Adolescent pregnancy and childbearing: Levels and trends in developed countries. *Family Planning Perspectives, 32*(1), 14–23.

Solomon, J., & Card, J. J. (2004). Making the list: Understanding, selecting, and replicating effective teen pregnancy prevention programs. Retrieved on November 23, 2004, from http://www.teenpregnancy. org

Taggart, R., & Lattimore, B. C. (2001). *Quantum opportunities program: A youth development program.* Los Altos, CA: Sociometrics.

# Chapter 9

Aspinwall, L. G., & Taylor, S. E. (1992). Modeling cognitive adaptation: A longitudinal investigation of the impact of individual differences and coping on college adjustment and performance. *Journal of Personality and Social Psychology, 63,* 989–1003.

Bandura, A. (1999). A social cognitive theory of personality. In L. Pervin & O. John (Eds.), *Handbook of personality* (2nd ed., pp. 154–196). New York: Guilford Press.

Barth, R. P. (1989). *Reducing the risk: Building skills to prevent pregnancy.* Santa Cruz, CA: ETR Associates/Network Publications.

Beck, M. S. (1991). *Increasing school completion: Strategies that work* (Monographs in Education No. 13). Athens, GA: University of Georgia College of Education.

Brooks-Gunn, J., & Furstenberg, F. F., Jr. (1986). The children of adolescent mothers: Physical, academic, and psychological outcomes. *Developmental Review, 6,* 224–251.

Burdell, P. (1998). Young mothers as high school students: Moving toward a new century. *Education and Urban Society, 30*(2), 202–223.

Clarke, G. (1992). Cognitive-behavioral group treatment of adolescent depression: Prediction of outcome. *Behavior Therapy, 23,* 341–354.

Codega, S. A., Pasley, B. K., & Kreutzer, J. (1990). Coping behaviors of adolescent mothers: An exploratory study and comparison of Mexican-Americans and Anglos. *Journal of Adolescent Research, 5*(1), 34–53.

Colletta, N. D., & Gregg, C. H. (1981). Adolescent mothers' vulnerability to stress. *Journal of Nervous and Mental Disorders, 169,* 50–54.

Coren, E., Barlow, J., & Stewart-Brown, S. (2003). The effectiveness of individual and group-based parenting programmes in improving outcomes for teenage mothers and their children: A systematic review. *Journal of Adolescence, 26*(1), 79–103.

de Anda, D., & Becerra, R. M. (1984). Social networks for adolescent mothers. *Social Casework: The Journal of Contemporary Social Work, 65,* 172–181.

DeBolt, M. E., Pasley, B. K., & Kreutzer, J. (1990). Factors affecting the probability of school dropout: A study of pregnant and parenting adolescent females. *Journal of Adolescent Research, 5*(3), 190–205.

Dupper, D. R. (1998). An alternative to suspension for middle school youths with behavior problems: Findings from a "school survival" group. *Research on Social Work Practice, 8*(3), 354–366.

D'Zurilla, T. J. (1986). *Problem-solving therapy: A social competence approach to clinical intervention.* New York: Springer.

D'Zurilla, T. J., & Nezu, A. (1982). Social problem-solving in adults. In P. C. Kendall (Ed.), *Advances in cognitive-behavioral research and therapy* (pp. 202–269). New York: Academic Press.

Fine, M. (1986). Why urban adolescents drop into and out of public high school. *Teachers College Record, 87,* 392–409.

Fischer, R. L. (1997). Evaluating the delivery of a teen pregnancy and parenting program across two settings. *Research on Social Work Practice, 7*(3), 350–369.

Franklin, C. (1992). Alternative school programs for at-risk youth. *Social Work in Education, 14*(4), 239–251.

Franklin, C., & Corcoran, J. (1999). Preventing adolescent pregnancy: A review of programs and practices. *Social Work in Health Care, 45*(1), 40–52.

Glodich, A., & Allen, J. G. (1998). Adolescents exposed to violence and abuse: A review of the group therapy literature with an emphasis on preventing trauma reenactment. *Journal of Child and Adolescent Group Therapy, 8*(3), 135–153.

Griffin, N. C. (1998). Cultivating self-efficacy in adolescent mothers: A collaborative approach. *Professional School Counseling, 1*(4), 53–58.

Harris, M. B., & Franklin, C. (2002). Effectiveness of a cognitive-behavioral group intervention with Mexican American adolescent mothers. *Social Work Research, 17*(2), 71–83.

Harris, M. B., & Franklin, C. (2004). Taking charge: A skills-based group intervention for adolescent mothers. Manuscript in review. New York: Oxford University Press.

Henshaw, S. K. (2004). *U.S. teenage pregnancy statistics with comparative statistics for women aged 20–24.* New York: Alan Guttmacher Institute.

Hogue, A., & Liddle, H. A. (1999). Family-based preventive intervention: An approach to preventing substance abuse and antisocial behavior. *American Journal of Orthopsychiatry, 69,* 275–293.

Jemmont, J. B., Jemmont, L. S., Fong, G. T., & McCaffree, K. (1999). Reducing HIV risk-associated sexual behavior among African American adolescents: Testing the generality of intervention effects. *American Journal of Community Psychology, 27*(2), 161–187.

Kalil, A., Spencer, M. S., Spieker, S. J., & Gilchrist, L. D. (1998). Effects of grand-mother coresidence and quality of family relationships on depressive symptoms in adolescent mothers. *Family Relations: Interdisciplinary Journal of Applied Family Studies, 47*(4), 433–441.

Larrivee, B., & Bourque, M. L. (1991). The impact of several dropout prevention intervention strategies on at-risk students. *Education, 112,* 48–63.

Maynard, R. A. (Ed.). (1997). *Kids having kids: Economic costs and social consequences of teen pregnancy.* Washington, DC: Urban Institute Press.

McWhirter, B. T., & Page, G. L. (1999). Effects of anger management and goal setting group interventions on state-trait anger and self-efficacy beliefs among high risk adolescents. *Current Psychology: Developmental, Learning, Personality, Social, 18*(2), 223–237.

Moore, K. A., Myers, D. E., Morrison, D. R., Nord, C. W., Brown, B. V., & Edmonston, B. (1993). The age of childbirth and later poverty. *Journal of Research on Adolescence, 3*(4), 393–422.

National Campaign to Prevent Teen Pregnancy. (2002). *Teen pregnancy: Not just another single issue.* Washington, DC: Author.

National Campaign to Prevent Teen Pregnancy. (2004). *Fact sheet: How is the 34% statistic calculated?* Washington, DC: Author.

Olah, A. (1995). Coping strategies among adolescents: A cross-cultural study. *Journal of Adolescence, 18*(4), 491–512.

Osofsky, J. D., Osofsky, H. J., & Diamond, M. O. (1988). The transition to parenthood: Special tasks and risk factors for adolescent parents. In G. Y. Michaels & W. A. Goldberg (Eds.), *The transition to parenthood: Current theory and research* (pp. 209–232). New York: Cambridge University Press.

Passino, A. W., Whitman, T. L., Borkowski, J. G., Schellenbach, C. J., Maxwell, S. E., & Keogh, D. R. (1993). Personal adjustment during pregnancy and adolescent parenting. *Adolescence, 28*(109), 97–123.

Pearson, L. C., & Banerji, M. (1993). Effects of a ninth-grade dropout prevention program on student academic achievement, school attendance, and dropout rate. *Journal of Experimental Education, 61*(Spring), 247–256.

Reid, W. J. (1996). Task-centered social work. In Francis J. Turner (Ed.), *Social work treatment: Interlocking theoretical approaches* (4th ed., pp. 617–640). New York: Free Press.

Rhodes, J. E., & Woods, M. (1995). Comfort and conflict in relationships of pregnant, minority adolescents: Social support as a moderator of social strain. *Journal of Community Psychology, 23*, 74–84.

Rice, K. G., & Meyer, A. L. (1994). Preventing depression among young adolescents: Preliminary process results of a psycho-educational intervention program. *Journal of Counseling and Development, 73*, 145–152.

Rodriguez, R. (1995). Latino educators devise sure-fire K–12 dropout prevention programs. *Black Issues of Higher Education, 12*, 35–37.

Sandfort, J. R., & Hill, M. S. (1996). Assisting young unmarried mothers to become self-sufficient: The effects of different types of early economic support. *Journal of Marriage and the Family, 58*(2), 311–326.

Stern, M., & Alvarez, A. (1992). Pregnant and parenting adolescents: A comparative analysis of coping response and psychosocial adjustment. *Journal of Adolescent Research, 7*(4), 469–493.

Stern, M., & Zevon, M. A. (1990). Stress, coping, and family environment: The adolescent's response to naturally occurring stressors. *Journal of Adolescent Research, 7*(4), 290–305.

Stramenga, M. S. (2003). The role of developmental and relational factors in the career decision-making process of adolescent mothers. *Dissertation Abstracts International: Section B: The Sciences and Engineering*, Vol. 64(6-B), 2962.

Vallarand, R. J., Fortier, M. S., & Guay, F. (1997). Psychosocial mechanisms underlying quality of parenting among Mexican-American and White adolescent mothers. *Journal of Personality and Social Psychology, 72*(5), 1161–1176.

Zeidner, M., & Hammer, A. L. (1990). Life events and coping resources as predictors of stress symptoms in adolescents. *Personality and Individual Differences, 11,* 693–703.

Zellman, G. L. (1981). *The response of the schools to teenage pregnancy and parenthood.* Santa Monica, CA: Rand.

Zupicich, S. (2003). Understanding social supportive processes among adolescent mothers. *Dissertation Abstracts International Section A: Humanities and Social* Sciences, Vol. 63(11-A), 3869.

# Index